LIVE BEAT

BEAT 4

WORKBOOK

T0345774

Rod Fricker • Ingrid Freebairn • Jonathan Bygrave • Judy Copage

Contents

1 LIFESTYLES				
	1a What are you doing here? p4	Present simple and present continuous Question tags	Clothes, styles, accessories and patterns	Shop for clothes
	1b I've loved every minute. p6	Present perfect simple with *for* and *since* Present perfect and past simple	Jobs	
	1c It's much more rewarding. p8	Intensifiers *much, far, a lot, a bit* with comparative adjectives and adverbs *(not) as … as*	Adjectives to describe work	
	1 Language round-up p10		**1 Skills practice** p11 SKILLS FOCUS: **READING** AND **WRITING**	

2 LIFE STORIES				
	2a I didn't recognise you. p12	Past simple Prepositions: *during, for*		Show concern and reassure
	2b I wasn't really listening … p14	Past continuous and past simple with *when, while, as*	Phrasal verbs with *up*	
	2c After getting up at 5 a.m., … p16	Past simple and past perfect simple *after/before* + gerund (*-ing* form)	Transport and travel	
	2 Language round-up p18		**2 Skills practice** p19 SKILLS FOCUS: **READING, LISTENING** AND **WRITING**	

3 RESPONSIBILITY				
	3a You'll sleep in tents. p20	Future tenses: *will, going to*, present continuous *to be about to* + infinitive	Food and kitchen equipment	
	3b I don't have to ask my parents. p22	*must, mustn't, should, ought to, have (got) to, don't have to, needn't, had better (not)* Gerund (*-ing* form) as subject and object	Part-time jobs	
	3c Please let me go. p24	*make, let, allowed to*		Invite, accept and refuse with excuses
	3 Language round-up p26		**3 Skills practice** p27 SKILLS FOCUS: **READING** AND **WRITING**	

4 ENTERTAINMENT				
	4a Phones which you can fold up … p28	Defining and non-defining relative clauses	Phrasal verbs with *on*	
	4b The most fun I've had for ages! p30	Present perfect simple with *just, already, before, never, ever, yet* Superlatives with the present perfect simple		React to good and bad news
	4c Ever since I was a child … p32	Present perfect simple and continuous with *for* and *since* Present perfect simple for numbers and amounts	Words connected with music	
	4 Language round-up p34		**4 Skills practice** p35 SKILLS FOCUS: **READING, LISTENING** AND **WRITING**	

5 NATURAL WORLD				
	5a Unless they do something, … p36	First conditional with *if, unless, provided that, as long as*	Landscape and natural environment	
	5b We won't know until we leave. p38	Future time clauses with *when, until, as soon as, by the time, before*	Extreme weather and natural disasters	
	5c In case it gets cold … p40	*in case* + present simple	Camping equipment	Make and respond to requests
	5 Language round-up p42		**5 Skills practice** p43 SKILLS FOCUS: **READING** AND **WRITING**	

6 IMAGINATION	**6a If you were invisible for a day,** ... p44	Second conditional with *would*, *might*, *could*	Transitive phrasal verbs	
	6b If only I had my camera! p46	*wish/if only* + past simple		Ask for and give advice
	6c We didn't mind queuing. p48	Verb with infinitive or gerund	Noun suffixes *-ion*, *-ment*, *-ity*, and *-y*	
	6 Language round-up p50		**6 Skills practice** p51 SKILLS FOCUS: **READING**, **LISTENING** AND **WRITING**	
7 COMMUNICATE	**7a He asked me if I had a website.** p52	Reported statements and questions		Phone messages
	7b You suggested getting a taxi. p54	Reported speech with verbs of reporting		
	7c In spite of your faults, ... p56	Clauses and linkers of contrast	Relationship words and phrases	
	7 Language round-up p58		**7 Skills practice** p59 SKILLS FOCUS: **READING** AND **WRITING**	
8 RIGHT OR NOT?	**8a He shouldn't have left it there.** p60	*should have/ought to have*		Apologise for past mistakes
	8b It can't be easy. p62	*must/can't/might/could* for deductions in the present	Phrasal verbs with *away*	
	8c He can't have drowned. p64	*must have/can't have/might have/ could have* for deductions in the past	Crime	
	8 Language round-up p66		**8 Skills practice** p67 SKILLS FOCUS: **READING**, **LISTENING** AND **WRITING**	
9 IN THE NEWS	**9a The telephone was invented.** p68	The passive: present simple, past simple, present perfect, past perfect	The media	
	9b They're being followed. p70	The passive: present continuous, past continuous and future simple		Give opinions, agree and disagree
	9c It ought to be stopped. p72	The passive: modals, gerund (*-ing* form) and infinitive	Adjective and noun formation	
	9 Language round-up p74		**9 Skills practice** p75 SKILLS FOCUS: **READING** AND **WRITING**	
10 MONEY	**10a If he had sold the ring,** ... p76	Third conditional with *would have*	Verbs connected with money	
	10b If only we'd had the money! p78	*wish/if only* + past perfect	Phrasal verbs with *out*	
	10c I might not have done so well. p80	Third conditional with *might have*		Give and accept congratulations
	10 Language round-up p82		**10 Skills practice** p83 SKILLS FOCUS: **READING**, **LISTENING** AND **WRITING**	

1a What are you doing here?

Phrases

1 ☆ **Choose the correct options.**

Max: Excuse me. I'm looking for a present for my girlfriend.

Assistant: What are you ¹**looking /** **after** **/** **wanting**?

Max: I'm not sure. ²**Something / Someone / Somewhere** unusual. I want to surprise her.

Assistant: How about some silver bangles?

Max: Oh, yes, these are great. Oh no! Here's my girlfriend now.

Laura: Hi, Max. How's it ³**coming / doing / going**?

Max: Laura! Hi! I thought you were at home.

Laura: No, I meet Sue here ⁴**every / each / all** other Saturday. We're going shopping today. I need some new clothes for my birthday party. ⁵**Anyway / However / Although**, what have you got there?

Max: Er … nothing, I … er …. Oh, is that the time? I must go. See you later.

Vocabulary: Clothes, styles, accessories and patterns

2 ☆ **Write the words.**

1 b_andana_   4 h_____   7 s_____   9 t_____ t_____

2 j_____   5 b_____   8 t_____   10 t_____ b_____

3 f_____-f_____   6 t_____   11 s_____

Grammar: Present simple and present continuous

3 ☆ **Choose the correct form of the verbs.**

FACESPACE GROUP

I love cool clothes!

Qu: Where ¹**do you usually shop /** **are you usually shopping** for clothes?

²**I always buy / I'm always buying** my clothes from the market. They ³**sell / are selling** the coolest (and cheapest) clothes.

Qu: What ⁴**do you wear / are you wearing** at the moment?

I'm at school at the moment. ⁵**I wear / I'm wearing** a fleece. The school is really cold today, so ⁶**I don't wear / I'm not wearing** cool clothes!

Qu: This is a question for the boys! ⁷**Do you ever wear / Are you ever wearing** bangles or ⁸**do you think / are you thinking** they are only for girls?

Well, ⁹**I wear / I'm wearing** some now. I wouldn't go to the shops and buy them, but sometimes ¹⁰**I borrow / I'm borrowing** my sister's!

Grammar: Question tags

4 ★★★ **Match the beginnings (1–10) with the question tags (a–l). There are two extra tags.**

1 That's the new boy,
2 He's from Scotland,
3 His sister's in Year 12,
4 They live near you,
5 Their dad doesn't live with them,
6 He works in America,
7 They've got a dog,
8 Your mum doesn't like it,
9 It tried to catch your cat,
10 And your mum called the police,

a) don't they?
b) does she?
c) is he?
d) haven't they?
e) isn't it?
f) didn't she?
g) does he?
h) isn't he?
i) have they?
j) didn't it?
k) isn't she?
l) doesn't he?

Use your English: Shop for clothes

5 ◄═► **Number the conversations in the correct order.**

Dialogue 1

	a) Beth:	Yes, please. I'm looking for a shirt.
[ ]	b) Beth:	It looks good. How much is it?
[1]	c) Assistant:	Can I help you?
[ ]	d) Beth:	That's a bit expensive. I'll leave it.
[ ]	e) Assistant:	How about this one?
[ ]	f) Assistant:	It's £25.

Dialogue 2

	a) Tim:	Can I try the black ones on?
[ ]	b) Tim:	Yes, please. Have you got these trousers in a different colour?
[ ]	c) Assistant:	Of course, the changing rooms are over there.
[ ]	d) Assistant:	Yes, we have. Black, red or brown.
[ ]	e) Assistant:	Do you need any help?

Grammar summary

Present simple and present continuous

Affirmative	Negative
I **live** in a small flat.	You **don't like** rock music.
She always **plays** tennis on Saturdays.	She **doesn't** often **go out**.
We**'re working** at the moment.	I**'m not eating** lunch now.
He**'s sleeping** at the moment.	It **isn't raining** at the moment.

Questions	Short answers
Do you often **go** to bed late?	Yes, I **do**. No, I **don't**.
Does she **like** fish?	Yes, she **does**. No, she **doesn't**.
Are they **cooking** dinner?	Yes, they **are**. No, they **aren't**.
Is he **getting** dressed?	Yes, he **is**. No, he **isn't**.

Wh- questions
What do you usually **do** on Saturdays?
What is she **doing** at the moment?

Note

Use
- We use the present simple to talk about permanent situations, routines and for timetabled events in the future.
  *They **live** in Greece.*
- We use the present continuous to talk about things that are happening now or around now.
  *My mum **is cooking** at the moment.*
- We don't usually use stative verbs in the present continuous, e.g. *like, love, hate, understand, know, want, believe.*
  *I **don't believe** in Santa Claus.*
  NOT ~~I'm not believing in Santa Claus~~.

Question tags

I'm late, **aren't I?**
You haven't got any money, **have you?**
He doesn't eat meat, **does he?**
Your parents are teachers, **aren't they?**

Note

Use
- We use question tags to check or confirm information.
  *You're in class 8C, **aren't you?***
- When we use a rising intonation, it shows that we aren't sure of the answer. When we use a falling intonation, it shows that we are simply checking something we already know.

1b I've loved every minute.

Vocabulary: Jobs

1 ⭐ **Rearrange the letters to make jobs.**

1 ufsehieow
   housewife

2 unsre
   _____

3 eiccmhna
   _____

4 hircaes
   _____

5 veeeidtct
   _____

6 atsjuronli
   _____

7 lubredi
   _____

8 lipto
   _____

9 iernegne
   _____

10 stirat
   _____

Grammar: Present perfect simple with for and since; Present perfect and past simple

2 ⭐ **Read the article and choose the correct options.**

HOW TO BECOME A STAR.

◀ Previous   **Become an extra**   ▶ Next

Extras are the people you see in the background of films or television programmes who don't speak. Thousands of people are needed every year, but is it a good way to become famous? Many people who ¹**have left** / left home years ago and ²**have gone** / went to Hollywood hoping to become stars ³**have been** / were there ⁴**for** / since many years and, so far, are still working as extras. No director ⁵**has noticed** / noticed them yet, but they still dream. Some are lucky. In four 1987 films, *Hunk, Less Than Zero, No Way Out* and *No Man's Land*, you may recognise one young extra. His name … Brad Pitt. Brad Pitt ⁶**has made** / made over fifty films ⁷**for** / since 1987 and is a huge star, but, back then, he ⁸**has been** / was just another hopeful extra. His parents ⁹**haven't been** / weren't actors and he ¹⁰**hasn't had** / didn't have any contacts or help with his career. A director ¹¹**has seen** / saw him, realised he had star quality and ¹²**has given** / gave him a chance.
So it can happen. Could it happen to you?

3 ⭐⭐ **Read the interview. Complete the questions and answers with the verbs in the present perfect or the past simple.**

INTERVIEW WITH AN EXTRA.
Danny Grantham is an extra on British TV.

◀ Previous   **Interview**   ▶ Next

1 Q: When _did you start_ (you/start) your career as an extra?
DG: _I started_ (I/start) in 2008.

2 Q: What _____ (be) your first part?
DG: _____ (I/be) a soldier in a programme about the First World War.

3 Q: What _____ (you/do) in that part?
DG: _____ (I/not/do) anything! I was in a hospital bed, asleep.

4 Q: How many programmes _____ (you/be) in altogether?
DG: Oh, that's difficult. _____ (I/be) in over one hundred programmes.

5 Q: _____ (you/ever/say) anything on screen?
DG: _____ (✓). _____ (I/say) 'Waiter' in a programme about a hotel!

6 Q: _____ (a director/ever/ask) you to play a bigger part in a programme?
DG: Yes. _____ (Three directors/offer) me parts, but I like being an extra. I'm not ready to be a real actor yet!

4 ⭐⭐ **Rewrite the sentences using the present perfect simple with for or since.**

1 I arrived here half an hour ago.
   I _'ve been here for half an hour_.

2 My parents got married twenty years ago.
   My parents _____.

3 Mr Burns started working at our school in September.
   Mr Burns _____.

4 Charles got his MP3 player last Tuesday.
   Charles _____.

5 I started dreaming of being a singer fifteen years ago.
   I _____.

5 ★★★★ **Make sentences from the prompts.**

Sean Connery

Shontelle

Nicole Kidman

Gianfranco Zola

1 Sean Connery/be/
   actor/1954
   *Sean Connery has been
   an actor since 1954.*

2 Before he/become/actor/
   he/be/lorry driver

   _____

   _____

3 Shontelle/study/
   law/when she/be/at
   university

   _____

   _____

4 She/know/Rihanna/they/
   be/at school together

   _____

   _____

5 Nicole Kidman/work for
   UNICEF/1994

   _____

   _____

6 In 2001, she/sing/
   'Something Stupid' with
   Robbie Williams

   _____

   _____

7 Gianfranco Zola/play/
   football/from 1984 to
   2005

   _____

   _____

8 He/be/a football
   manager/2006

   _____

   _____

Grammar summary

Present perfect and past simple

Affirmative	Negative
I**'ve seen** that film three times.	He **hasn't found** a job yet.
I **saw** that film last week.	He **didn't** find a job last summer.

Questions	Short answers
Have you ever **acted** in a play?	Yes, I **have**. No, I **haven't**.
Did you **act** in a play last year?	Yes, I **did**. No, I **didn't**.

Wh- questions
Where have you **been**?
Where did you **go** last night?

Note

Use

- We use the present perfect simple to connect past events with the present.
  - a past experience at an unstated time
    *I**'ve lived** in Madrid.*
  - recent actions with a present result
    *I**'ve washed** my dad's car.*
  - things which started in the past and are still true now
    *I**'ve known** Mick for five years.*
    *I**'ve been** here since two o'clock.*
- We use the past simple to talk about events which are finished.
  *I **worked** in a shop for three months.* (I don't work there now.)

Present perfect simple with *for* and *since*

I've had this **for** two years.
We've lived here **for** six months.
He's worked here **since** September.
They've been married **since** 2007.

Note

Use

- We use the present perfect simple with *for* and *since* to show how long an action or event has been in progress. We use *for* with a period of time and *since* with a point in time.
  *We've been here **for** three hours.*
  *We've been here **since** three o'clock.*

1c It's much more rewarding.

Vocabulary: Adjectives to describe work

1 ⭐ **Complete the adjectives to describe the jobs.**

1 d<u>ull</u>, b _ _ _ l _ -p _ _ _ d

2 d _ _ g _ r _ _ _ _ , e _ c _ _ _ _ n _

3 g _ _ _ m _ _ o _ _ _ , w _ _ _ _ -p _ _ _ _

4 w _ _ _ t _ w _ _ _ _ _ _ , r _ w _ _ d _ _ _ _

2 ⭐⭐ **Choose the correct options.**

This is a great opportunity. It's very ¹⃞creative⃞ / **dull** / **stressful** as you can use your artistic skills to make each burger different! You meet new people every day and the job can be very ²**educational** / **exciting** / **tiring** when a famous film star or singer comes in for a burger. The green and yellow uniform is very ³**glamorous** / **rewarding** / **worthwhile** and the job is also ⁴**dangerous** / **well-paid** / **educational** as you will learn exactly how many fries there are in a 100g portion. Come and apply now!

It's a ⁵**stressful** / **badly-paid** / **interesting** job – only 50p an hour! The work is ⁶**exciting** / **glamorous** / **dull** – the same thing all day, every day. It's also ⁷**tiring** / **safe** / **educational** as you are on your feet all day. It can be ⁸**rewarding** / **creative** / **dangerous**, too – three people burnt themselves last week!

Grammar: Intensifiers *much, far, a lot, a bit* with comparative adjectives and adverbs; *(not) as … as*

3 ⭐ **Choose the correct options.**

1 Teachers aren't as badly-paid [as] / than / like nurses.

2 Cleaners work **more hard / harder / more hardly** than shop assistants.

3 You should think about your work **careful / more careful / more carefully**.

4 Please drive **slower / more slow / more slowly**!

5 My new job is **easier / more easy / more easily** than my old one, but it isn't as **good- / well- / better-**paid.

6 I earn **fewer / worse / less** than you and I work a **lot / far / much** longer than you each day.

7 Why aren't you as **happy / happily / more happy** as I am?

8 I'm getting **a bit / far / a lot** more money than last year, but not much.

4 ⭐⭐ **Compare the activities using the information given.**

✓✓ much more	= as … as
✓ a bit more	✗ not as … as

BACKPACKING/DOING VOLUNTARY WORK

1 doing voluntary work ✓✓ backpacking (difficult)
Doing voluntary work is much more difficult than backpacking.

2 doing voluntary work ✓ backpacking (interesting)
_____

3 backpacking ✗ doing voluntary work (dangerous)
_____

4 backpacking = doing voluntary work (rewarding)
_____

5 doing voluntary work ✓✓ backpacking (useful)
_____

Grammar summary

Intensifiers *much, far, a lot, a bit* with comparative adjectives and adverbs; *(not) as … as*

Teaching is **much more rewarding** than office work.
Acting is **far more stressful** than writing.
Working in a factory is **a lot duller** than working in an office.
Being a lawyer is **a bit better-paid** than being an accountant.
We work **a lot more quietly** now than we used to.
My dad doesn't explain things **as clearly as** my mum does.

Note

Use

- We use intensifiers with comparative adjectives and adverbs to show how similar or different two things are.
  *I work **a bit** harder than my sister.*
  *I work **a lot** harder than my sister.*

- We use *(not) as … as* to say that two things are or are not the same. We often use *not as … as* to avoid using a negative adjective.
  *I'm **as clever as** my sister.*
  *My brother is **not as** clever **as** I am.*
  NOT ~~My brother is more stupid than I am.~~

Common mistakes

~~I drive slower than my sister.~~ ✗
I drive **more slowly** than my sister. ✓
~~Summer work isn't as hard to find like normal work.~~ ✗
Summer work isn't as hard to find **as** normal work. ✓

1 Language round-up

1 Complete the words.

Clothes

1 l_e_g_gin_g_s
2 f __ __ __ c __
3 t __ g __ t __

Styles

4 s __ __ __ p __ d
5 b __ g __ __
6 c __ __ c __ __ d

Accessories

7 b __ __ g __ e
8 b __ n __ __ n __
9 h __ __ r b __ __ d

Adjectives to describe jobs

10 g __ __ m __ __ o __ s
11 w __ __ t __ w __ __ l __
12 e __ __ c __ t __ __ n __ __

.../11

2 Match the beginnings (1–11) to the endings (a–k).

1 John isn't here,
2 Have you
3 They don't work here,
4 Do you
5 Is being a waiter more interesting
6 Are you
7 You've been here before,
8 Have you been here since
9 Have you known her for
10 Is your new job as well-paid
11 How long have you had

a) believe me?
b) a long time?
c) working at the moment?
d) is he?
e) this morning?
f) as your old one?
g) than working in a shop?
h) seen this film?
i) that watch?
j) haven't you?
k) do they?

.../10

3 Complete the sentences with the correct form of the auxiliaries *have*, *do* or *be*.

1 Where _do_ you live?
2 You like football, _____ you?
3 _____ Stephen know Emily?
4 Who _____ Pia talking to at the moment?
5 Mark _____ written any emails yet.
6 Your mum _____ speak French, does she?
7 I'm going to school by bus today, _____ I?
8 How much money _____ you spent so far today?
9 This isn't your phone, _____ it?
10 What _____ you do last night?

.../9

4 Complete the text with the correct form of the words from the box.

- as • since • be • tall • high • know
- far • talented • fast • for • appear

Jaime Nared has played basketball [1]_since_ she was four years old. She [2]_____ several times on television and is famous in the USA.

Jaime is amazing. Even when she was young, she was much [3]_____ than her school friends – in fact, at the age of thirteen, she was [4]_____ tall as a lot of eighteen year olds and she was always [5]_____ better at basketball than children of her own age. She could run much [6]_____ and no one could jump as [7]_____ as she could.

Before she went to High School, Jaime played for Team Concept, a girls' basketball team. The trainer there, Michael Abraham [8]_____ a basketball trainer [9]_____ over thirty years. He [10]_____ how difficult it can be for very talented young players to find other people of their own age to compete against and how important it is that they can play in a team where everyone is as [11]_____ as they are.

.../10

LISTEN AND CHECK YOUR SCORE

Total	.../40

1 Skills practice

SKILLS FOCUS: READING AND **WRITING**

Read

1 **Match the headings (1–4) to the correct texts (A–D).**

1 A shopping centre ☐   3 Jumble sales ☐

2 A market ☐   4 Charity shops ☐

A

My parents are members of a local theatre group and they often organise these to raise money. I always help them because, as I'm sorting out the bags of clothes that people give us, I often find something for myself. I always pay for them, but nothing costs more than 50p!

B

I rarely buy new clothes. These shops are great for finding unusual old jackets, trousers and shirts that people don't want anymore. They're really cheap and the money you spend all goes to people who need help. There are three in our main shopping street.

C

My friends and I usually get the bus here on Saturdays. It's great. There are 130 shops, four restaurants and a cinema. Some of the shops are quite expensive, but there are often sales so you can usually find some good bargains.

D

This is a great place to buy clothes. I love walking around the different stalls. The only problem is that there are no changing rooms so, if you want to try things on, everyone can see you! It's OK for jackets and jumpers, but not so easy if you want to buy trousers.

2 **Read the texts again. Answer true (T), false (F) or doesn't say (DS).**

1 Text A: The speaker's parents do a lot of acting.   *DS*

2 Text A: The best thing about helping is that you don't have to pay for the clothes that you find.   ___

3 Text B: The clothes sold here are not new.   ___

4 Text C: The girl and her friend usually go to the cinema after shopping.   ___

5 Text D: You can't try clothes on here because there are no changing rooms.   ___

Write

3 **Complete the article with the words from the box.**

> • looks • buys • see • wearing
> • boots • market • wears • usually
> • dressed • ~~cool~~

A friend whose fashion style I admire.

The friend I want to write about is Nicola. She always wears really [1]*cool* clothes and she [2]_____ great whatever she has on.

Nicola loves [3]_____ hats. You never [4]_____ her without one on her head. Sometimes she wears women's sun hats, but [5]_____ she wears old-fashioned men's hats like you see in gangster films! She [6]_____ a mixture of styles. Last week, she came to school [7]_____ in a summer dress with a man's jacket and a pair of old walking [8]_____.

Nicola usually [9]_____ her clothes from the [10]_____. She goes there every Saturday and she spends hours looking for interesting new things to wear.

4 **You are going to write a similar article about one of your friends. Before you start, organise your ideas.**

clothes/accessories he/she wears

_____

_____

adjectives to describe his/her look

_____

_____

other information (where he/she buys his/her clothes, etc.)

_____

_____

5 **Now write the article.**

A friend whose fashion style I admire.

The friend I want to write about is …

11

Phrases

1 Complete the dialogues with phrases from the box. There is one extra phrase.

> • Do you fancy • You'll get the hang of it • ~~No problem~~ • I bet you're glad
> • I'd better get going • I could do with

1 **Russ:** I'm sorry I'm late.

 Tim: *No problem*. No one else has arrived.

2 **Liz:** Beth said the film was awful last night.

 Debbie: _____ you didn't go.

3 **Pete:** I'll never play the guitar well.

 John: Don't worry. _____. Just keep practising.

4 **Dave:** What time's your train?

 Ed: Nine o'clock. _____ or I'll miss it.

5 **Ben:** Hi, Luke. Do you want something to eat?

 Luke: No thanks, I'm not hungry, but _____ a glass of water. It's really hot today.

Grammar: Past simple

2 Complete the text with the past simple form of the verbs in brackets.

Shaun White ¹*was* (be) born in 1986 in California. At the age of five, doctors ² _____ (discover) a problem with his heart. After that, he ³ _____ (have) two successful operations. He was always interested in sport, but he ⁴ _____ (not start) snowboarding until he was thirteen years old. It ⁵ _____ (not take) him long to win his first competition.
He ⁶ _____ (win) silver in the Winter X Medals competition in 2002, but then he ⁷ _____ (not win) another silver medal until 2007. Why not? Because, from 2003 to 2006, he ⁸ _____ (come) first in every competition. The only medals he ⁹ _____ (win) were gold! He also ¹⁰ _____ (go) to Turin for the 2006 Winter Olympics and ¹¹ _____ (return) home with another gold medal.
Shaun is now a multimedia star. There's a DVD about his Olympic success, a snowboarding documentary and there was even a joke about him in the film *Ocean's 13*!

3 Complete the internet chat with the correct form of the verbs from the box.

> • come • see • win • forget • ask
> • go • not go • not have • not watch
> • not be • ~~see~~

Chats | Friends | Profile

Hi, Tim.

Hello, Nick. ¹*Did* you *see* the snowboarding last night?

No, I didn't. I ² _____ all about it. ³ _____ Shaun White _____?

No, he ⁴ _____ second. I can't believe that you ⁵ _____ it. You love snowboarding.

I know, but I ⁶ _____ time yesterday. I ⁷ _____ at home last night.

Really? Where ⁸ _____ you _____?

To the cinema.

What film ⁹ _____ you _____?

A romantic comedy.

What? You hate romantic comedies.

I know, but I ¹⁰ _____ alone. I was with Melanie Stevens.

No way! Tell me all about it. When ¹¹ _____ you _____ her out?

Well …

Grammar: Prepositions: *during* and *for*

4 ⭐ **Choose the correct options.**

Q: Hi, Paul. When did you start windsurfing?

A: I started ¹**for** / **during** the summer holidays two years ago. My family went to Italy ²**for** / **during** two weeks and I had lessons there.

Q: Now that it's warm, you can go windsurfing again. What did you do ³**for** / **during** the winter?

A: Most of the time I was at school! I wanted to go somewhere warm ⁴**for** / **during** the holidays, just ⁵**for** / **during** a few days, but it was too expensive. I went windsurfing once in the sea near where I live. I did it ⁶**for** / **during** about five minutes then I fell in the water. It was freezing!

Use your English: Show concern and reassure

5 ⭐ **Choose the correct options.**

Dialogue 1

Mum: What on ¹**the world** / **earth** / **the planet** happened to you?

Jason: I ²**fall** / **fell** / **feel** off my bike. A car went past really quickly and I lost my ³**balance** / **weight** / **wheels**.

Mum: Did you ⁴**hurt** / **pain** / **damage** yourself?

Jason: No, don't ⁵**mind** / **hurry** / **worry**. I'm fine, but my bike isn't!

Dialogue 2

Dad: Are you ⁶**OK** / **right** / **good**?

Louise: Yes. I had an accident on my skateboard. My knee hurts a bit, but it's nothing.

Dad: Can I ⁷**do** / **help** / **find** anything?

Louise: No, I'm fine.

Dad: Are you ⁸**real** / **sure** / **worry**?

Louise: Yes, well … OWW! … can you help me to the sofa?

Dad: OK. No ⁹**surely** / **really** / **problem**.

Grammar summary

Past simple

Affirmative	Negative
I **dropped** my phone yesterday. We **went** to the cinema last night.	They **didn't move** house last year. He **didn't eat** his pizza yesterday.
Questions	Short answers
Did you **work** last summer? **Did** she **find** her purse?	Yes, I **did**. No, I **didn't**. Yes, she **did**. No, she **didn't**.

Wh- questions
Who did you **talk** to at the party? **What did** you **do** last night?

Note

Use

- We use the past simple to talk about single, completed actions in a completed time period in the past.
  *I **went** to a party last Friday.*
- We can use the past simple without a time expression when the speaker and listener both know what the time period is.
  ***Did** you **see** the Real Madrid match?* (on television last night)

Prepositions: *during* and *for*

I met my friends **during** the summer holidays.
We went on holiday **for** two weeks.

Note

Use

- We use *during* to say when something happened and *for* to say how long it lasted.
  *I felt ill **during** the exam.*
  *I was in hospital **for** a week.*

Common mistakes

My phone rang while the exam. ✗
My phone rang **during** the exam. ✓

2b I wasn't really listening ...

Vocabulary: Phrasal verbs with *up*

1 ⭐ **Choose the correct options.**

Hi Mel,

I'm back. The summer camp was awful! Every day was the same: we had to wake up at 6 a.m! Honestly! I'm not ¹**taking** / **turning** / **making** it up. We had to tidy our bedrooms before breakfast! We had to ²**take** / **grow** / **pick** up all the clothes from the floor and then make our beds.

As for meal times! Well, we had breakfast at 7.30 then we didn't eat again until we had lunch at 1 p.m. I was always hungry! And guess what! When the teachers came in to the dining room, we all had to ³**stand** / **get** / **pack** up until they sat down.

Oh, and you know I only went so I could go windsurfing? Well, I ⁴**made** / **gave** / **took** up after one lesson. I hated it!

I'll tell you more when I see you. How was your holiday?
Cath

Hi Cath,

⁵**Cheer** / **Give** / **Look** up! You're home now! Luckily, I had a great time. I really wanted to do something new, so I ⁶**found** / **looked** / **picked** up some activities on the internet. In the end, I ⁷**worked** / **made** / **took** up go-karting. I was worried that it would be very crowded, but only five people ⁸**took** / **came** / **turned** up on the first day. We didn't have to wait for a free kart. It was great! I went every day for two weeks and really enjoyed it.

See you soon,
Mel

Grammar: Past continuous and past simple with *when, while, as*

2 ⭐ **Complete the text with the past continuous or the past simple form of the verbs in brackets.**

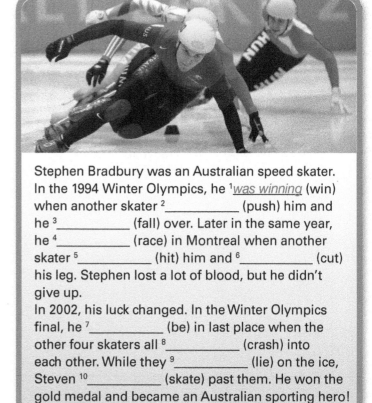

Stephen Bradbury was an Australian speed skater. In the 1994 Winter Olympics, he ¹*was winning* (win) when another skater ²_____ (push) him and he ³_____ (fall) over. Later in the same year, he ⁴_____ (race) in Montreal when another skater ⁵_____ (hit) him and ⁶_____ (cut) his leg. Stephen lost a lot of blood, but he didn't give up.
In 2002, his luck changed. In the Winter Olympics final, he ⁷_____ (be) in last place when the other four skaters all ⁸_____ (crash) into each other. While they ⁹_____ (lie) on the ice, Steven ¹⁰_____ (skate) past them. He won the gold medal and became an Australian sporting hero!

3 ⭐⭐ **Write sentences with *when*, *while* or *as* and the past continuous or the past simple. Do not change the order of the words.**

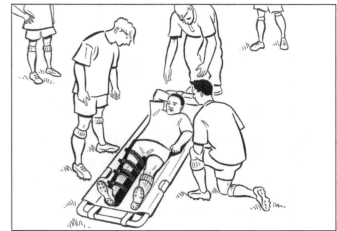

1 Connor/break leg/play football

   Connor *broke his leg while/as he was playing football*.

2 Molly's phone/ring/take an exam

   Molly's phone _____.

3 I/use/my friend's computer/it crash

I _____.

4 Joe/walk near Loch Ness/see 'the monster'

Joe _____.

5 Charlotte meet the cool, handsome French boy/she not know/what to say

_____.

4 🔊 **Use the prompts to complete the dialogue. Use the past continuous or the past simple and add *when*, *while* or *as* if necessary.**

Paula: Hi, Beth. We had a pretty normal day at school today, but Mr Smith was really angry with us.

Beth: Why?

Paula: ¹We/not sit/quietly/he/come in.
We weren't sitting quietly when he came in.

Beth: ²What/you/do?

_____

Paula: ³I/read/a book,

_____

but other people weren't so quiet.

Beth: ⁴Tom and Mike/fight?

_____

Paula: ⁵✓ _____ As usual!
⁶Mr Smith/come/in, some people/not hear/him.

_____

_____

The room slowly got quieter and quieter as people noticed him. Nick was looking out of the window. He was the last one to notice Mr Smith.

⁷he turn/round, everyone else/sit/at their desks.

_____

_____

Beth: ⁸What/he/do?

_____

Paula: He went bright red and quickly sat down!

Grammar summary

Past continuous and past simple with *when, while, as*

While/As I **was walking** home, I **saw** an accident.
I **saw** an accident **while/as** I **was walking** home.
When I **left** home, my dad **was eating** breakfast.
My dad **was eating** breakfast **when** I **left** home.

Past simple + past simple with *when*

When Tom **stood up**, his bag **fell** on the floor.
Tom's bag **fell** on the floor **when** he **stood up**.

Note

Use

- We use the past continuous and past simple together to talk about an action that happened while another action was in progress. We use the past continuous for the longer action and the past simple for the shorter finished action.
  *I **was working** when my friend **arrived**.*

- We use *while/as* before the past continuous. We use *when* before the past simple. When we start a sentence with *when*, *while* or *as*, we separate the two clauses with a comma.
  ***While** we **were swimming**, it **started** raining.*

- Sometimes we can see the same activities as an activity in progress or a single event. We can choose which tense to use.
  ***While** I **was cooking** dinner, my friend **did** his homework.*
  *I **cooked** dinner **while** my friend **was doing** his homework.*

- We can use past simple + past simple with *when* if two actions occur at the same time in the past.
  *I **felt** ill **when** I **got** up*

Common mistakes
~~We were playing while the teacher came into the room.~~ ✗
*We were playing **when** the teacher came into the room.* ✓

Vocabulary: Transport and travel

1 Complete the words.

Dear Parent/Carer,

Summer camp
The summer camp this year is going to take place near Lake Fairview. There will be a chance for students to ¹w*alk* on paths in the forests, ²s_____ on the lake in a yacht and ³r_____ bikes and horses. We can take forty-five students ⁴b_____ coach. If any parents would like to ⁵d_____ to the camp, please could you let us know if it would be possible for one or two students to get a ⁶l_____ with you?
Thank you.
Yours
Jane Preston, Head teacher.

Dear Rachel,
I'm in pain in Spain! My mum and dad don't realise how tall I am. We ⁷f_____ here on a cheap plane with very small seats and then we got the smallest car my dad could find! I can't get ⁸i_____ or ⁹o_____ very easily and I have to sit in the back because my mum feels sick if she isn't in the front. It's really uncomfortable and we keep going on long journeys in the countryside! Luckily, today we got bikes and ¹⁰c_____ in the forest and, in the evening, we went by bus to a castle. It was lovely to get ¹¹o_____ and ¹²o_____ without any problems!

To: Martha Jason
From: Ron Smith, manager
Please find attached your tickets to Berlin. As you can see, you haven't got plane tickets. You are going by train. You have to ¹³c_____ trains in Paris. The train from England comes into the Gare du Nord and the train to Berlin leaves one hour later from the Gare de l'Est. Don't worry. They are very close to each other. You won't need a taxi. You can go on ¹⁴f_____.

Grammar: Past simple and past perfect simple

2 Look at the pictures and complete the sentences with the verbs in the past simple or the past perfect simple.

1 When Bob *arrived* (arrive) at the station, the train *had left* (leave).

2 When David _____ (get) to school, the lesson _____ (start).

3 By the time Mark _____ (turn up) at the party, all the food _____ (go).

4 When Paula _____ (open) her school bag, she _____ (realise) that she _____ (leave) her books at home.

5 The car _____ (crash) into the tree because the driver _____ (fall) asleep.

6 Phil _____ (forget) to switch off his mobile phone before the film _____ (start).

3 ⭐⭐⭐ **Complete the text with the past simple or the past perfect simple form of the verbs from the box.**

> • come • fly • ask • catch • get • give
> • make • spend • arrive • happen • take

When Samantha Lazarris booked her holiday to Costa Rica she didn't expect to arrive in Puerto Rico!

When she asked a taxi driver at the airport to take her to her hotel in San Juan, he laughed. He told her that she ¹*had come* to the wrong country. How ² _____ it _____? Samantha's travel agent ³ _____ a mistake. Samantha ⁴ _____ for a ticket to San José, the capital of Costa Rica. However, the travel agent ⁵ _____ her a ticket to San Juan, the capital of Puerto Rico. San Juan is 1,800 kilometres from San José!

Samantha finally ⁶ _____ in San Juan, very tired and much poorer. She ⁷ _____ £800 of her own money to get there. First, she ⁸ _____ to Miami in the USA. Then she ⁹ _____ a plane to San Juan. The journey from San José to San Juan ¹⁰ _____ four days.

Now everyone is asking the same question. How ¹¹ _____ she _____ on the plane without realising that it was going to the wrong country?

Grammar: *after/before* + gerund (*-ing* form)

4 ⭐ **Complete the sentences with the correct form of the verbs in brackets.**

1 After *getting* (get) off the plane, we got a taxi to central London.

2 Before _____ (go) on the London Eye, we booked into our hotel.

3 After _____ (buy) some French bread, we climbed the Eiffel Tower.

4 Before _____ (leave) Rome, we visited the Coliseum.

5 After _____ (fly) to Athens, we got a boat to a Greek island.

6 Before _____ (return) home, we spent a week on the beach.

Grammar summary

Past simple and past perfect simple

By the time Jack **arrived**, his friends **had left**.
By the time Maria **started** university, she **had saved** over £500.
I **hadn't heard** any Jet songs until my friend **gave** me their CD for my birthday.
A: Nick **came** home really late last night.
B: Really? Where **had** he **been**?

Note

Use

• We use the past perfect with the past simple to show that one past action or event happened before another.
• We often use the past perfect when the order of the events is not clear.
  *When I **woke** up, my parents **went out**.* (They went out after I woke up.)
  *When I **woke** up, my parents **had gone out**.* (They went out before I woke up.)

Common mistakes
~~I felt tired because I stayed up all night playing computer games.~~ ✗
*I felt tired because I **had stayed** up all night playing computer games.* ✓

after/before + gerund (*-ing* form)

After finishing his homework, Ben **wrote** his blog.
Before buying a new computer, I **looked** at prices on the internet.

Note

Use

• We can use *after/before* + *-ing* instead of the past simple or past perfect.
  *After I **had eaten**, I went out.*
  After eating, I went out.
• We can only use *after/before* + *-ing* + past simple when the subject is the same in both parts of the sentence.
  *After failing my exams, **I** started working harder.* ✓
  ~~After failing my exams, my mum was very angry.~~ ✗
  *After **I** failed my exams, **my mum** was very angry.* ✓

2 Language round-up

1 Choose the correct options.

Hi Steve,

I'm in Budapest. I came [1]**by** / **on** / **with** coach.
We [2]**had left** / **left** / **were leaving** London at
2 p.m. on Thursday and arrived at 6 p.m. on
Friday! Before [3]**left** / **had left** / **leaving** England,
I [4]**was buying** / **bought** / **had bought** an MP3
player so I had something to listen to [5]**for** /
during / **while** the journey.
[6]**When** / **While** / **During** we left London, no one
was sitting next to me and I had two seats
[7]**during** / **for** / **on** a long time. Then we stopped
in Germany and some more people got on.
A woman sat next to me. She [8]**carried** / **had**
carried / **was carrying** a huge bag of food. After
[9]**took** / **taking** / **had taken** off her coat, she sat
down and got out some sandwiches. I [10]**hadn't**
eaten / **didn't eat** / **wasn't eating** since London
and I was really hungry. I [11]**was looking** / **looked** /
had looked at her eating when she [12]**had invited** /
was inviting / **invited** me to eat with her. It was
delicious! Now, I'm getting ready to go out and see
the city.
See you soon.
Jack

.../11

2 Complete the questions and answers.

1 A: you/go/the cinema/yesterday?

   Did you go to the cinema yesterday?

   B: ✗ I/go/the theatre.

   _____

2 A: you go very fast/you/fall off/your bike?

   _____

   B: ✗ I/cycle/quite slowly.

   _____

3 A: your parents/go to bed by the time you/get
      home/last night?

   _____

   B: ✗ They/wait/for me in the living room.

   _____

4 A: John say 'Hello'/you meet/him yesterday?

   _____

   B: ✓ We/have/a long chat together.

   _____

.../14

3 Complete the texts with the words from the box.

• drives   • fly   • changing   • lift   • cheers
• ride   • take   • in   • stand   • by   • off
• gave   • foot   • turn   • makes   • on

I hate [1]*changing* trains when there isn't much
time. First you worry that your train will be late.
Then you get [2]_____ the first train and try
to find the second one. You have to run and there
are always lots of people in the way. When you
get [3]_____, it's full of people and you have
to [4]_____ up for the whole journey. Even
worse, it isn't there and doesn't [5]_____ up
at all. I'd rather go [6]_____ bus.

When it's raining, I get a [7]_____ to school
from my dad, but, usually, I go on [8]_____.
I used to [9]_____ my bike, but a lot of bikes
were stolen from our school, so I [10]_____
up before my bike disappeared, too.

I'd like to [11]_____ up sailing. My friend sails
every weekend. He's seventeen and he's got his
own car so he [12]_____ to the lake. It's a
really cool car and when he gets [13]_____
and sits there, he's like the king of the road!

My friend sometimes [14]_____ up stories.
She told us that her dad could [15]_____ a
plane and we all believed her. She usually does
it when she's upset. I think it [16]_____
her up and I feel sorry for her, but it's annoying
sometimes.

.../15

🎧 LISTEN AND CHECK YOUR SCORE	
Total	.../40

2 Skills practice

SKILLS FOCUS: READING, LISTENING AND WRITING

Read

1 **Read the texts. Match the topics (1–5) to the texts they appear in.**

1 A car journey _B_   4 A plane journey ___

2 A ferry journey ___   5 A tunnel   ___

3 A train journey ___

A

Dear Gran and Grandpa,

We're in Copenhagen. It's a beautiful city. We flew to Malmö with a budget airline, but the best part of the journey was the train ride from Malmö to Copenhagen on the Oresund bridge-tunnel. It's fantastic. From Malmö, it's a bridge. It's fifty-seven metres above the sea. Then, in the middle of the sea, there's an island called Peberholm and the bridge turns into a tunnel.

We're going to see the Little Mermaid and Tivoli Gardens today, but the bridge is the best.

See you soon!

Danny

B

Dear Aunt Eileen,

We're in Italy. We got the ferry to France and Dad's driven all the way here. Yesterday, we were in Chamonix in France and this morning we drove through the road tunnel under Mont Blanc. It was amazing. It's eleven kilometres long and goes from Chamonix in France to Courmayeur in Italy. It took eight years to build it. Now we're in Aosta. There are lots of things to see here and we had a real Italian pizza for lunch! Tomorrow we're going to Verona. Then, no more driving for a week!

Love, Mel

2 **Read the texts again and complete the summary with one word in each gap.**

Danny [1]_flew_ to Malmö and then went by

[2]_____ to Copenhagen. There's a

[3]_____ from Malmö to the [4]_____ of

Peberholm and then there is a [5]_____ to

Copenhagen.

Mel's dad [6]_____ to Italy. They got to

Italy through a tunnel which is [7]_____

kilometres long. Their plan is to drive all the way

to [8]_____, but they aren't there yet.

Listen

3 🎧 **Listen to the talk and complete the names with the words from the box. There are three extra words.**

- Francis • Golden • Silver • Duck • Hind
- Drake • Head

Boat: The _____ _____

Man: Sir _____ _____

4 🎧 **Listen again and complete the sentences with one word, number or date in each gap.**

The boat left England in [1]_December_ 1577.

In the spring of 1578, they arrived in [2]_____.

They got home on September 26th, [3]_____.

The boats were carrying stolen [4]_____.

The new boat has also been around the

[5]_____.

The new boat has been in London since

[6]_____.

The boat had twenty-two [7]_____ and could

sail at [8]_____ kilometres an hour.

Write

5 **Complete the article with the correct form of the verbs from the box.**

- set • start • attack • die • ~~be~~ • fight
- have • return (x2) • sail

Sir Francis Drake [1]_was_ born in 1540. He

[2]_____ eleven brothers and [3]_____

sailing when he was quite young. By the time he

[4]_____ off on his journey around the world,

he [5]_____ already _____ to America

several times. He [6]_____ also _____

Spanish boats and stolen their gold, so it was no

surprise when he [7]_____ home from his

journey with a fortune in Spanish gold.

After [8]_____ home, Francis Drake became

a politician. He also [9]_____ in the war

against Spain from 1585–1588. He [10]_____

near Panama in Central America in 1596 and his

body has never been found.

Vocabulary: Food and kitchen equipment

1 ⬜⭐ **Look at the pictures and complete the table.**

Cutlery	Crockery	Kitchen utensils
		1 sieve

Grammar: Future tenses: will, going to, present continuous

2 ⬜⭐ **Choose the correct options.**

Annie: Hi, Olivia. Where are you going?

Olivia: I'm going shopping. I've got £20 and ¹**I'm going to buy** / **I'll buy** two CDs.

Annie: Which ones?

Olivia: I don't know, but I'm sure ²**I'll find** / **I'm finding** something. What about you?

Annie: ³**I'll meet** / **I'm meeting** Kate at the market. ⁴**We'll go** / **We're going** to a party next Saturday so we want to buy something nice. ⁵**We're going to look for** / **We'll look for** some cool T-shirts. I saw a great one last time I was there, but I bet it isn't there today!

Olivia: Well, ⁶**you'll have** / **you're having** fun looking around anyway.

Annie: Why don't you come with us?

Olivia: No, it's OK. ⁷**I'm not going to stay** / **I won't stay** in town long. As soon as I've got my CDs, I have to go home. My dad's boss and his wife ⁸**will come** / **are coming** for dinner. I'm sure my mum ⁹**will be** / **is being** nervous so ¹⁰**I'm helping** / **I'm going to help** her with the cooking.

3 ⬜⭐⭐⭐ **Complete each dialogue with the correct form of the verbs. Use *will*, *going to* and the present continuous in each dialogue.**

1 • help • make • have

Emily: What are you doing this afternoon, Dad?

Dad: I '*m going to make* a cake.

Emily: Why?

Dad: Have you forgotten? It's your mum's birthday tomorrow and we '*re having* a party.

Emily: Oh, yes! I '*ll help* you if you like.

Dad: Thanks. You can wash the cake tin.

2 • stop • play • watch

Ryan: I'm tired. I think I _____ working for a while and rest.

Ben: I _____ the football later. Chelsea _____ Barcelona. Let's watch it together.

Ryan: OK, great.

3 • do • be • leave

Dad: Right, we _____ on Saturday for our holidays and there's a lot to do before then. It _____ a busy week. Your mum and I can't do everything.

Hannah: I _____ the washing and ironing if you like and then I can pack the clothes.

Dad: Great. What about you, Tim?

4 • not talk • meet • spend

Mum: Callum, Dan wants to go to the cinema with you.

Callum: Oh, Mum! I _____ my friends there. Do I have to take him?

Mum: Don't be so mean. He _____ to you or your friends. He just wants to see the film.

Callum: But we want to do something after the film. We _____ the whole evening together. How will Dan get home?

Grammar: *to be about to + infinitive*

4 ☆☆ **Read the information and complete the sentences with the correct *be about to* form of the verbs from the box.**

Dad is getting into the car.

Mum is filling the kettle with water.

My brother is putting his coat on.

My sister is cutting some bread.

My grandmother is holding a tin opener.

My uncle and aunt are getting out the kitchen scales.

I am going into the bathroom.

The students are sitting nervously in the classroom waiting for the teacher to give them their exam papers.

> • go • find out • open • have
> • ~~drive~~ • weigh • make (x2)

1 Dad *is about to drive* to work.

2 Mum _____ a cup of tea.

3 My brother _____ to school.

4 My sister _____ some sandwiches for lunch.

5 My grandmother _____ a tin of tuna.

6 My uncle and aunt _____ some food.

7 I _____ a shower.

8 The students _____ their exam results.

Grammar summary

Future tenses: *will, going to*, present continuous	
Affirmative	**Negative**
I**'ll (will) meet** you outside the cinema.	He **won't (will not)** travel by plane.
They**'re going to buy** a new computer this year.	She **isn't going to study** English.
We**'re meeting** Mark at three o'clock.	I**'m not going to** the cinema this week.
Questions	**Short answers**
Will they **travel** by car?	Yes, they **will**.
	No, they **won't**.
Are we **going to watch** a DVD?	Yes, we **are**.
	No, we **aren't**.
Are you **staying** in a hotel in Spain?	Yes, we **are**.
	No, we **aren't**.
Wh- questions	
What will you **do**?	
Where are you **going to go**?	
Who are you **meeting**?	

> **Note**
>
> **Use**
> - We use *will* to talk about something we think, believe or know will happen in the future. We can use *will be* for future facts.
>   *I'll be twenty-one in 2020.*
> - We can use *will* when we suddenly decide to do something.
>   *The rain's stopped. I think I'll go out.*
> - We use *going to* for plans, intentions and predictions in the future based on present evidence.
>   *I'm going to eat more healthily from now on.*
> - We use the present continuous for fixed plans and arrangements in the future.
>   *I'm playing volleyball for the school tomorrow afternoon.*
> - We can often use more than one future form.
>   Prediction: *You'll have/You're going to have a great time in Italy.*
>   Arrangements: *I'm meeting/I'm going to meet John later.*
> - When we use *going to* with the verb *to go*, we usually omit *to go*.
>   *I'm going ~~to go~~ shopping later.*

to be about to + infinitive

Quick! The film **is about to start**.

You can't get a drink now. Our train **is just about to leave**.

> **Note**
>
> **Use**
> - We use *to be (just) about to* + infinitive to talk about things that are going to start very soon.
>   *I can't talk now, I'm just about to go out.*

3b I don't have to ask my parents.

Vocabulary: Part-time jobs

1 ⬛ **Match the beginnings of the job adverts (1–8) to the endings (a–h).**

1 If you like animals, you should try dog   a) grass.

2 Two fit young people needed to cut   b) tables.

3 We need friendly, smart young people to serve in our   c) shop.

4 Local newsagent needs boys and girls for early morning newspaper   d) decorating.

5 Work with us stacking   e) walking.

6 Help others by teaching   f) computer skills.

7 Earn good money waiting at   g) shelves.

8 Just moved house? We'll do your painting and   h) deliveries.

Grammar: Gerund (-ing form) as subject and object

2 ⬛ **Complete the sentences using the gerund (-ing form) of the verb.**

1 It isn't easy to teach English.

   Teaching English isn't easy.

2 It's fun to take dogs for a walk.

   I love _____ dogs for a walk.

3 It's boring to serve customers in a shop.

   _____ customers in a shop is boring.

4 It's hard work to stack shelves.

   _____ shelves is hard work.

5 It's great to earn money by working part-time.

   _____ money by working part-time is great.

6 It's horrible to get up early in the morning.

   I don't like _____ early in the morning.

Grammar: *must, mustn't, should, ought to, have (got) to, don't have to, needn't, had better (not)*

3 ⬛ **Look at the information about a part-time job and complete the sentences with *should*, *shouldn't*, *have to* or *don't have to*.**

```
(◄) (►) [                              ] (✕)

PART-TIME JOBS – YOUR OPINIONS OF THE
GOOD, THE BAD AND THE UGLY!

DOG WALKING (Your rating ★★★★☆)

Good things
1 No uniform
2 Not inside all day

Bad things
3 Early starts
4 Cleaning up!

Advice
5 Make sure you're fit
6 No more than two dogs at one time!
```

1 You _don't have to wear_ (wear) a uniform.

2 You _____ (work) inside.

3 You _____ (get up) early.

4 You _____ (clean up) when your dog makes a mess!

5 You _____ (be) fit.

6 You _____ (take) more than two dogs at one time.

22

4 🔊 Complete sentences 1b–10b so that they mean the same as sentences 1a–10a. Use the words in brackets.

Advice for
PAPER ROUNDS

1a It is necessary to get up early. (must)
1b *You must get up* early.

2a You'll need to buy a good bike. (better)
2b _____ a good bike.

3a You can have your MP3 player on because there's no one to listen to or talk to. (don't have to)
3b _____ or talk to anyone so you can have your MP3 player on.

4a My advice is to watch out for dogs in people's gardens. (ought to)
4b _____ for dogs in people's gardens.

5a It's not a good idea to go to bed late. (shouldn't)
5b _____ to bed late.

6a You can wear your old clothes – no one expects you to look smart. (don't have to)
6b _____ smart.

7a Don't throw the newspapers on the ground – that only happens in American films. (mustn't)
7b _____ the newspapers on the ground.

8a Remember that even when it's raining you can't stay in bed. (have to)
8b _____ even when it's raining.

9a It's a good idea to take a mobile phone with you. (should)
9b _____ a mobile phone with you.

10a Don't worry – it's a great job. (needn't)
10b _____ – it's a great job!

Grammar summary

Gerund (-ing form) as subject and object

Watching TV is a waste of time.

> **Note**
>
> **Use**
> - We can use the gerund (-ing form) when the word is the subject of a sentence.
>   *Walking is healthy.*
> - We can sometimes use the gerund when the word is the object of a sentence. We use it after certain verbs and prepositions.
>   *I hate **skiing**.*

must, mustn't, should, ought to, have (got) to, don't have to, needn't, had better (not)

Obligation
You **must try** harder next year.
You **mustn't be** rude to your friends.
I **have to be/'ve got to be** at school at 8.30 tomorrow.

No obligation
We **don't have to/needn't** pay for the hotel until we arrive.

Advice
You **should wear** something smart to the interview.
You **ought to do** more exercise.
We**'d better** leave soon.
You**'d better not be** late for school again.

> **Note**
>
> **Use**
> - We use *must* and *have (got) to* for obligations and things that are necessary.
>   *We **have to wear** a uniform.*
> - We often use *must* when an obligation comes from the speaker.
>   *I **must get** my hair cut.*
> - We use *mustn't* to talk about things that we can't do and with negative obligations.
>   *You **mustn't eat** here.*
> - *must* and *have to* have different meanings in negative sentences: *don't have to* = no obligation; *mustn't* = it's against the rules.
>   *I **don't have to go** to school today.*
> - We use *should/shouldn't* and *ought to/ought not to* for giving advice, making suggestions and saying what is right and wrong.
>   *You **ought to do** more exercise.*
> - We use *needn't* when something is not necessary.
>   *You **needn't rush**.*
> - We use *had better (not)* to give slightly stronger advice. It often suggests that if you don't follow the advice, there could be a problem.
>   *You**'d better not be late** again.*

3c Please let me go.

Grammar: make, let, allowed to

1 ⭐ **Choose the correct options.**

1 My mum *makes* me tidy my room every
   Saturday.
   a) lets   b) makes   c) allows

2 I'm ___ to stay up late on Fridays and
   Saturdays.
   a) let   b) made   c) allowed

3 Are pupils in your school ___ to wear what they
   like?
   a) allowed   b) let   c) made

4 Our teacher ___ us stay late yesterday because
   we hadn't finished our work.
   a) made   b) allowed   c) let

5 Will your parents ___ you come to the concert
   with us on Friday evening?
   a) make   b) let   c) allow

6 My dad ___ me watch TV before I do my
   homework, but my mum doesn't.
   a) allows   b) lets   c) makes

7 My parents don't ___ me to stay at my friend's
   house all night.
   a) let   b) make   c) allow

8 I won't ___ my brother use my computer again.
   It's really slow now.
   a) let   b) allow   c) make

2 ⭐ **Make sentences from the prompts.**

1 I/not allow/go out/on schooldays
   I'm not allowed to go out on schooldays.

2 On Fridays my parents/let/stay out/until 11 p.m.
   _____

3 They/make/tidy my room/once a week
   _____

4 They/not make/do any other housework
   _____

5 We/not allow/wear/jeans to school
   _____

6 My mum/let/wear earrings, but she/not let/wear
   make-up
   _____

3 ⭐ **Complete the text about Summerhill School with the correct form of the verbs in brackets.**

Summerhill School was opened in Suffolk,
east England in 1921. It looks like a traditional
school, but, in many ways, it is very different. The
students [1](allow/decide) *are allowed to decide*
how the school should be run and what the rules
should be. The school [2](let/do) _____
the students _____ whatever they want
as long as they don't hurt others. The teachers
[3](not make/go) _____ the students
_____ to lessons, the students [4](allow/
choose) _____ which classes
they attend.
Students and teachers have meetings three
times a week. The students [5](allow/discuss)
_____ their ideas and are
equally as important as the teachers. There are
some things that the students [6](not allow/do)
_____, but the punishments
for breaking the rules are also decided by both
teachers and students. For example, they [7](make/
wait) _____ a student _____ until
last before they can get their dinner or they [8](not
let/leave) _____ a student _____
the school when everyone else [9](allow/go)
_____ out.
The British government does not always agree
with the ideas at Summerhill and it has, in the
past, tried to [10](make/change) _____ the
school _____ how it educates students. So
far, the school has continued to do what it thinks
is best.

Use your English: Invite, accept and refuse with excuses

4 🔊 **Choose the correct options.**

Mia: Do you ¹[want]/ **like** / **love** to go to the cinema this evening?

Sophie: I'd ²**want** / **wish** / **like** to, but I'm ³**worried** / **afraid** / **nervous** I can't. It's my mum's birthday.

Mia: That's a shame. What ⁴**for** / **about** / **of** tomorrow?

Sophie: Yes, that ⁵**sounds** / **looks** / **feels** great.

5 🔊 **Complete the dialogue with the words from the box. There are three extra words.**

> • love • would • want • can't • afraid
> • got • sounds • fancy • sorry • really
> • ~~over~~

Liam: Can you come ¹*over* this afternoon?

Adam: Yes, I'd ²_____ to.

Liam: Good. I've got to clear my grandparents' garden and I need some help.

Adam: Oh … er. I've just remembered. I'm ³_____ sorry, but I ⁴_____ come today.

Liam: No? Why not?

Adam: Well, I … er. I've ⁵_____ to look after my brother.

Liam: You haven't got a brother! I understand. You don't really ⁶_____ gardening.

Adam: It's hard work!

Liam: My grandparents are going to buy me a pizza and give me £10. So, what do you think? Do you ⁷_____ to help?

Adam: Pizza and cash! That ⁸_____ great. OK, I'll be there soon.

Grammar summary

make, let, allowed to

Affirmative

My dad **makes me clean** my shoes every day.
My parents **let me watch** TV for one hour a day.
I'm **allowed to wear** what I like at the weekend.

Negative

My parents **don't make me help** with the cooking.
My mum **doesn't let me** go out during the week.
I'm **not allowed to eat** fast food.

Note

Use

• We use *make* to talk about things we are told we have to do.
  *My parents **make me tidy** my room.*

• We use *let* and *allowed to* to talk about things that someone says we can do.
  *Our teacher **lets us go** home early.*
  *We are **allowed to drink** water in lessons.*

Form

• We can use *make* and *allowed to* in the active and passive forms.
  *My parents **make me go** to bed at 10 p.m./*
  *I am **made to go** to bed at 10 p.m.*
  *My parents **allow me to stay** up late./*
  *I am **allowed to stay** up late.*

• *Let* doesn't have a passive form.
  *My mum **lets me stay** out late.* ✓
  NOT ~~I'm let stay out late.~~

Common mistakes

~~I'm not allowed wear jewellery.~~ ✗
*I'm not allowed **to** wear jewellery.* ✓
~~My parents don't let me to stay out late.~~ ✗
*My parents don't **let me stay** out late.* ✓

3 Language round-up

1 Choose the correct options.

1 I want to get better marks so **I'm going to work harder** / **I'll work harder** next year.

2 **I'll meet** / **I'm meeting** my friends outside the cinema at six o'clock.

3 He made **us do** / **us to do** a test on Friday.

4 My parents didn't let **me go** / **me to go** out on Wednesday evening.

5 We're not allowed **use** / **to use** our phones.

6 We're just about **to have** / **having** lunch.

7 I don't fancy **to go** / **going** out tonight.

8 She **made** / **let** me sit at the front of the class.

9 You ought **be** / **to be** more careful.

10 Come in. Don't worry. You **mustn't** / **don't have to** take your shoes off.

11 You're not **let** / **allowed** to swim here.

12 Hurry up. **You're being** / **You'll be** late.

…/11

2 Complete the text with the phrases from the box.

- going on • I should take • will be
- have to study • knives, forks and spoons
- allowed to go • is going to bring • I'll have
- make me study • bowls, plates and saucers
- let me go • just about to start

We're ¹*going on* a camp next week. Everyone
²_____ something. I'm taking
cutlery – ³_____. Beth is
taking crockery – ⁴_____.
I think the weather ⁵_____
nice, but Mum won't ⁶_____
without a coat! I'm surprised I'm
⁷_____ at all. We're
⁸_____ our exams
at school and my parents usually
⁹_____ all the time. I know
I'll ¹⁰_____ when I get back.
Maybe ¹¹_____ my books with
me? No! Bad idea! ¹²_____ a
rest and then study.

…/11

3 Complete the dialogue with one word in each gap.

A: I've got a summer job. They need more people.
Do you ¹f*ancy* coming with me? I'm just
²a_____ to go and see the boss.

B: That ³s_____ great. I need some money.
What kind of job is it?

A: Lots of things. Grass ⁴c_____,
⁵w_____ on tables in a restaurant, a bit
of painting and ⁶d_____. I just have to
do what they tell me to do. The best thing is
that I'm ⁷a_____ to use the swimming
pool for free when I'm not working.

B: Where is it?

A: The Beachfront holiday camp. There are
bedrooms to tidy, there's a shop – you could
⁸s_____ customers there or
⁹s_____ shelves in the evening. Come
with me and see the boss. You don't
¹⁰h_____ to decide now. You can talk to
your parents and phone him tomorrow.

…/9

4 Choose the correct options.

Hi Harry,

I've just got a new part-time job on Saturdays. I
wash cars. It's great. I ¹**mustn't** / **don't have to** /
ought to get up early because I don't start work
until 2 p.m. I ²**needn't** / **have to** / **don't have
to** clean the cars inside and outside. ³**I'll** / **I'd
better** / **I'm going to** work on Sundays as well
to earn more money. By the summer holidays,
⁴**I'm having** / **I'll have** / **I must have** about £500,
which is great. ⁵**I'm going** / **I'd better go** / **I'll go**
to Greece with my parents and ⁶**I'm spending** /
I'm going to spend / **I have to spend** my money
on diving lessons.

Anyway, I hope all is well. ⁷**I'll** / **I'd better** / **I
mustn't** go because we are ⁸**about to** / **must** /
going have lunch and I'm not ⁹**let** / **allowed** /
made to be late.

See you,

Matt

P.S. You ¹⁰**ought** / **should** / **must** to get a
weekend job. It's good to earn money.

…/9

LISTEN AND CHECK YOUR SCORE	
Total	…/40

3 Skills practice

SKILLS FOCUS: READING AND WRITING

Read

1 **Read the text and number the paragraphs in the correct order.**

A ☐

Most of this aid has come through the Yéle Haiti Foundation, which he created in 2004 with his cousin. Yéle means 'a cry for freedom' and Yéle Haiti aims to help people in Haiti with small projects that can provide them with work, food and somewhere to live. Wyclef wants Haitians to be able to live in their own country and not to have to become refugees to survive.

B ☐

Wyclef Jean was born in Haiti, a poor island in the Caribbean, in 1972. When he was nine years old, his family moved to the USA. He grew up in New Jersey where he met Pras Michel, another Haitian, and Lauren Hill, an African-American. Together, they formed a band in the mid 1990s. They called their band The Fugees, a short form of the word 'refugees', because all of their families had come to the USA to look for a better life. As well as being a successful musician, Wyclef spent a lot of time giving humanitarian help to his homeland.

C ☐

Wyclef has had a lot of support for his foundation from other show-business stars. Brad Pitt and Angelina Jolie attended the first anniversary party for Yéle Haiti. After Hurricane Ike hit the island in 2008, Matt Damon went to Haiti to serve food to the people who had lost their homes in the storm. Wyclef's story shows that people who leave their own country can sometimes give something back to help the people who are left behind.

2 **Read the text again and answer the questions.**

1 When and where was Wyclef born?
   In Haiti in 1972.

2 Where did he grow up?
   _____

3 Why was the band named The Fugees?
   _____

4 What does Yéle mean?
   _____

5 What did Matt Damon do to help the people of Haiti?
   _____

Write

3 **Imagine that you and your family have moved to Great Britain. You have been there for one month. Think about these questions and use your imagination to make notes.**

1 Where do you now live?
   _____
   _____

2 What's your new school like?
   _____
   _____

3 Have you made any friends?
   _____
   _____

4 What do you do in your free time?
   _____
   _____

5 What are the main differences between life at home and life in Britain?
   _____
   _____

4 **Write a letter to a friend telling him/her about your new life. Use your notes from Exercise 3.**

Hi … ,
I'm sorry I haven't written before. I'm now living in …

Grammar: Defining and non-defining relative clauses

1 ⭐ **Are the relative clauses defining (D) or non-defining (ND)?**

1 This is the magazine which had a photo of me on the front cover last month. _D_

2 Tom Hayden, who's fifteen on Saturday, is going to have a party at his house. ___

3 My aunt, whose husband is German, is moving to Bonn soon. ___

4 I'm looking for a book that is easy to read and has an exciting story. ___

5 Is this the shop where you bought your cool T-shirt? ___

6 We're going to Alnwick Castle, which was Hogwarts School in the Harry Potter films. ___

2 ⭐ **Choose the correct options.**

Search 🔍

Don't get too excited!

Most people ¹**which / who / what** own a computer have also got a printer. Now, newspapers and websites are full of stories of 3D printers, ²**what / which / who** they say can make an exact copy of anything. People ³**what / who / whose** read these stories may believe that, by buying a printer, they may never have to go shopping again.

According to Tom Jenkins, ⁴**who / which / whose** job is to create 3D objects, this is not quite true. Firstly, printers ⁵**who / which / whose** can make large and complicated objects are very expensive, as are the materials they use. Secondly, the objects ⁶**that / what / who** can be made are not finished and need a lot of work to make them strong enough to use. Thirdly, although there are websites ⁷**which / where / whose** you can find 3D designs, you really need to understand design to be sure your objects are going to work.

Tom compares 3D printers to bread making machines, ⁸**where / who / which** were popular a few years ago. People ⁹**which / whose / who** bought them soon found that they were paying more for the ingredients and spending more time making the bread than they would by buying bread from their local supermarket.

3 ⭐⭐⭐ **Rewrite the sentences in the dialogue using the words in brackets.**

Andy: I've just found a new social networking site. It's really good. (which)

1 I've just found _a new social networking site which is really good_.

Aaron: How did you hear about it?

Andy: Ryan Davies told me. His brother's in my class. (whose)

2 Ryan Davies, _____ _____.

Aaron: What's so special about this site?

Andy: There's a cool forum. You can post anything you want there. (where)

3 There's a cool forum _____ _____.

I was on one before. It wasn't as good as this one. (that)

4 I was _____ _____.

Aaron: I don't like putting my personal details on a webpage. Anyone can see them. (where)

5 I don't like _____ _____.

Andy: You can stop people seeing your personal details if they aren't your friends. (who)

6 Only people _____ _____.

Aaron: How many friends have you got on it?

Andy: I've only got seventeen friends so far. It isn't many. (which)

7 I've only got _____ _____.

I've only been on it a day, though!

Vocabulary: Phrasal verbs with *on*

4 ⭐ **Look at the pictures and complete the words.**

1 You have to log on to use this website.

2 Can I t_____ these on, please?

3 Andy and Jake g_____ on very well and always walk to school together.

4 I'll answer the phone. You c_____ on with your meal. Don't let it go cold.

5 H_____ on, I'll just go and get him.

6 Quick! S_____ on the TV! Our school is on the news today.

Grammar summary

Relative clauses

Defining relative clauses

people **(who/that)**
He's the guitarist **who/that** played on Eminem's last album.

places **(where)**
This is the place **where** we first met.

things **(which/that)**
Is this the jumper **which/that** you wanted to buy?

possessions **(whose)**
This is the girl **whose** friends have made a CD.

Non-defining relative clauses

people **(who)**
My dad, **who** is a teacher, always checks my homework.

places **(where)**
The hotel, **where** we stayed last summer, was in the city centre.

things **(which)**
This CD, **which** I bought last week, is really good.

possessions **(whose)**
Jackie Dawes, **whose** mum sometimes appears on TV, wants to be an actress.

Note

Use

- We use defining relative clauses with *who/that*, *where*, *which/that* or *whose* to add essential information to a clause so that it is clear what we are talking about.
  *These are the people **whose** house we rented last summer.*

- We use non-defining relative clauses with *who*, *where*, *which* and *whose* to add extra information to a sentence. This information is not essential to the understanding of the sentence and the sentence still makes sense if you remove the non-defining relative clause.
  *Mr and Mrs Smith, **whose** house we rented last summer, were very kind to us.*

Form

- In defining relative clauses when *who*, *which* or *that* refers to the object, we can miss it out.
  *This is the town **(which)** my dad was born in.*
  It is not possible to miss out *whose* or *where*.
  *I met a boy **whose** dad was an actor.*

- A non-defining relative clause is separated from the main information by a comma, or if it is in the middle of a sentence, two commas.
  *Johnny Depp, **who** played Captain Jack Sparrow in Pirates of the Caribbean, is a good guitarist.*

4b The most fun I've had for ages!

Phrases

1 ⭐ **Match the statements (1–5) to the responses (a–e).**

1 I'm not sure I can do this.

2 Let's go to the fair. We might win something.

3 I'm going to have another go.

4 I'm going to the beach. Are you up for it?

5 This game looks quite difficult.

a) Oh no you're not! It's my turn now.

b) No, it's dead easy. Just throw the dart at the playing card.

c) Well, have a go. You won't know until you try.

d) Don't get too excited. The prizes aren't usually that great.

e) Yes, great. I'll just go and get my swimming things.

Grammar: Present perfect simple with *just, already, before, never, ever, yet*

2 ⭐ **Make sentences from the prompts. Use the present perfect simple.**

1 you/already/win/three!

You've already won three!

2 we/not try/this/yet.

Come on! _____

_____

3 we/just/have/a burger.

No way. _____

_____

4 I/never/be/on it before.

I don't know. _____

_____

5 your husband/ever/climb/a wall like this? _____

_____

6 I/not see/him before.

I don't know. _____

_____

3 ⭐⭐⭐ **Complete the chat with the present perfect simple form of the verbs in brackets and the time expression in the correct place.**

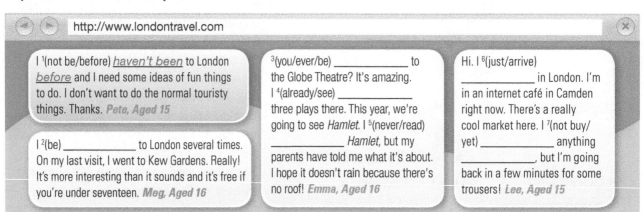

http://www.londontravel.com

I ¹(not be/before) *haven't been* to London *before* and I need some ideas of fun things to do. I don't want to do the normal touristy things. Thanks. *Pete, Aged 15*

I ²(be) _____ to London several times. On my last visit, I went to Kew Gardens. Really! It's more interesting than it sounds and it's free if you're under seventeen. *Meg, Aged 16*

³(you/ever/be) _____ to the Globe Theatre? It's amazing. I ⁴(already/see) _____ three plays there. This year, we're going to see *Hamlet*. I ⁵(never/read) _____ *Hamlet*, but my parents have told me what it's about. I hope it doesn't rain because there's no roof! *Emma, Aged 16*

Hi. I ⁶(just/arrive) _____ in London. I'm in an internet café in Camden right now. There's a really cool market here. I ⁷(not buy/ yet) _____ anything _____, but I'm going back in a few minutes for some trousers! *Lee, Aged 15*

Grammar: Superlatives with the present perfect simple

4 ⭐ **Complete the questions with the correct form of the words in brackets.**

1 What's _the best_ (good) place you _'ve ever been_ (ever/be) to?

2 What's _____ (big) prize your sister _____ (ever/win)?

3 What's _____ (tasty) food you _____ (ever/eat)?

4 What's _____ (good) computer game you _____ (ever/play)?

5 What's _____ (boring) book your mum _____ (ever/read)?

6 Who's _____ (nice) person you _____ (ever/meet)?

Use your English: React to good and bad news

5 ⭐ **Complete the dialogues with one letter in each gap.**

1 **Max:** My parents have just booked a holiday in New York for this summer.

 James: Wow! That's am_a_z_i_ng !

 Kate: How fant_a_sti_c_!

2 **Leo:** Oh no, I've forgotten my homework.

 Anna: Oh dear! That's t __ __ b __ d. You worked all weekend on it.

 Sean: N __ __ __ r m __ __ d. You can bring it tomorrow.

3 **Ellie:** I can't believe it! Someone's stolen my phone.

 Mel: That's a __ __ __ l.

 Harry: How t __ __ r __ __ __ e.

4 **Jack:** Mum and Dad bought me an electric guitar for my birthday.

 Victoria: That's really c __ __ l!

 Helen: That's b __ __ l __ __ __ __ t! When's your first concert?

5 **William:** I won first prize in the school essay competition.

 Charles: Good f __ r y __ __. You deserve it!

 Harry: W __ __ l d __ __ e. You worked really hard on your essay.

Grammar summary

Present perfect simple with *just, already, before, never, ever, yet*

Affirmative

I**'ve just finished** my exam.
We**'ve seen** this film already.

Negative

Mark **hasn't played** the guitar in a concert **before**.
Tom **has never failed** an exam.
I **haven't phoned** Beth **yet**.

Questions

Have you **ever had** an accident at school?
Has the concert started **yet**?

Note

Use

- We use the present perfect with
  - *just* to show that something happened a very short time ago.
  - *already* in affirmative sentences to emphasise that something has happened before.
  - *before* in negative sentences to say that this is the first time something has happened.
  - *never* in affirmative sentences to mean 'not ever'. We often add *before* to emphasise the sentence.
  - *ever* in questions when we ask *Have you ever…?* to mean 'at any time in your life'.
  - *yet* at the end of questions and negatives to mean 'until now'.

Form

See Unit 1, page 7

Common mistakes

~~I haven't never seen so much food.~~ ✗
I**'ve never** seen so much food. ✓

Superlatives with the present perfect simple

This is the **best** present I**'ve ever had**.
What's the **hottest** place you**'ve been** to?

Note

Use

- We use superlatives with the present perfect simple to talk about the best/biggest/worst thing that has ever happened to us.

4c Ever since I was a child ...

Grammar: Present perfect simple and continuous with *for* and *since*

1 ⭐⭐ **Complete the sentences. Use the present perfect simple or continuous and *for* or *since*.**

1 They (play) *have been playing* together *for* thirty years.

2 We (look) _____ for Tom's house _____ three o'clock this afternoon. Let's stop and ask someone.

3 It's our anniversary. I (go out) _____ with Emma _____ a year.

4 'When did you meet?' 'Oh, a long time ago. We (know) _____ each other _____ primary school.'

5 It's broken. I (have) _____ only _____ it _____ Tuesday.

6 Where is she? We (wait) _____ here _____ four hours.

2 ⭐⭐ **Complete the questions and answers with the present perfect simple or continuous. Use *for* and *since* where necessary.**

Jennifer and Bradley ⭐⭐⭐
The new Tom and Meg?

[1]People/enjoy/Tom Hanks and Meg Ryan films/'Joe Versus the Volcano' in 1990.
People have been enjoying Tom Hanks and Meg Ryan films since 'Joe Versus the Volcano' in 1990.
Now Hollywood has found a new Meg and Tom – Jennifer Lawrence and Bradley Cooper.

Q: [2]How long/Jennifer/act?

_____

A: [3]She/act/she was fourteen.

_____

Q: [4]How long/she/make/films?

_____

A: [5]She/make/films/about six years.

_____

Q: [6]How long/Jennifer and Bradley/know each other?

_____

A: [7]They/know/each other/they met at dancing lessons for the film 'Silver Linings Playbook'.

_____

Q: [8]How long/they/go out/with each other?

_____

A: [9]They/never/go out/together! (not yet!)

_____

Grammar: Present perfect simple for numbers and amounts

3 ⭐ **Complete the questions with the verbs from the box in the present perfect simple.**

- ~~make~~ • produce • appear • be • score
- win • sell

Quick star quiz

1 **Q:** How many albums _have_ Limp Bizkit _made_?
A: Five.

2 **Q:** How many Oscars _____ Meryl Streep _____?
A: Three.

3 **Q:** How many CDs _____ U2 _____?
A: More than 150 million!

4 **Q:** How many people _____ in the band Metallica since 2003?
A: Four.

5 **Q:** How many episodes of _Hannah Montana_ _____ her father _____ in?
A: Well, he wasn't in three episodes …

6 **Q:** How many goals _____ David Beckham _____?
A: I think it's over 250. He got 91 in 2012.

7 **Q:** How many songs _____ Eminem _____?
A: A lot. The best was _Renegade_ by Jay-Z.

Vocabulary: Words connected with music

4 Complete the crossword and find the hidden word.

1 Kanye West is a _rapper_.

2 My favourite _____ on the CD _Some Nights_ by _Fun_ is _We are Young_.

3 I think _Irreplaceable_ by Beyoncé is a great _____.

4 Do you think One Direction are a better _____ than The Wanted?

5 There are ten songs on our new _____.

6 Look! We're number one in the _____.

7 The best selling _____ since the year 2000 is _Hips Don't Lie_.

8 The _____ to Robbie Williams's songs are always interesting.

Crossword:
1 R A P P E R
2 T
3 S
4 B
5 A
6 C
7 S
8 L

Grammar summary

Present perfect simple and continuous with _for_ and _since_

Present perfect simple

I**'ve known** Maria **for** three years.
Have you **known** her **for** a long time?
Have you **known** her **since** you were children?

Present perfect continuous

Tim**'s been playing** the guitar **since** he was seven.
Have you **been waiting** here **for** a long time?
Has he **been playing** the guitar **since** he was a young boy?

Note

Use

- We use the present perfect simple and continuous with _for_ and _since_ to show the duration of an action or event.
- We use _for_ with a period of time up to the present.
  I've been here **for** ten minutes.
  We've been waiting **for** an hour.
- We use _since_ to show the exact point of time in the past when the action or event started.
  Henry's been going out with Jane **since** last year.
  We've been studying for our exams **since** April.

Form

- To form the present perfect continuous we use _have/has_ + _been_ + gerund (_-ing_ form) of the verb.
  I **have been sitting** here for ten minutes.

Common mistakes

~~How long have you been knowing your best friend?~~ ✗
How long have you **known** your best friend? ✓
~~I've read this book for five days.~~ ✗
I've **been reading** this book for five days. ✓

Present perfect simple for numbers and amounts

Connie **has won lots** of prizes for her school work.
Matt **has written three** books.
How many exams **have** you **taken** so far this week?

Note

Use

- We use the present perfect simple to answer the question _How much/many_ in unfinished time periods, e.g. in your life, this week.
  **How many** countries have you been to? (in your life)
  **How many** albums have you made? (since the band started)

4 Language round-up

1 Complete the text with a word or phrase from the box. Put the verbs in the correct form.

> • do • ever • have • amazing • buy • sell
> • not leave • most exciting • scratch • just
> • yet • wash • ~~start~~

John Edwards and Jack Watson [1]_started_ to make money when they were eleven! So, what [2]_____ they _____? They [3]_____ people's cars! Now, at just eighteen, they are successful businessmen and they [4]_____ school [5]_____!
Since last year, they [6]_____ and selling electrical equipment. 'We buy stuff that people [7]_____ or damaged,' said John 'and then sell it.'
This year, they [8]_____ already _____ 800 TVs to a company in Spain and an English university has [9]_____ bought 1,000 from them, too. 'It's the [10]_____ thing we've [11]_____ done,' they said.
If you think that's [12]_____, why not [13]_____ a go yourself?

.../12

2 Complete the questions with the correct form of the words in brackets.

1 What's _the best_ (good) film you've ever seen?
2 How long _____ (you/wait)?
3 How many James Bond films _____ (you/see)?
4 How much money _____ (your brother/save) for his holiday?
5 _____ (you/listen) to the CD yet?
6 _____ (you/ever/read) any books by George Orwell?
7 How long _____ (you/know) William?
8 What's _____ (bad) meal you've ever eaten?
9 _____ (you/work) here long?
10 How long _____ (she/have) that bag?

.../9

3 Complete the text with one word in each gap.

Do you want your own website? Have you got an idea [1]w_hich_ is going to make you rich? Well [2]h_____ on! We're here to give you advice. We have [3]b_____ working in web design [4]f_____ more than twenty years. [5]C_____ on us for reliable advice!
We have more than 100 articles about starting a business, [6]w_____ is more than any other website. We have experts, [7]w_____ advice is easy to read and always useful. You will find special sections [8]w_____ you can see what your designs will look like.
If you are already a member, [9]l_____ on with your username and password below. People [10]w_____ aren't members can join by clicking here.

.../9

4 Complete the texts with one letter in each gap.

Amanda Ghost, [1]_w h o s e_ real name is Amanda Louisa Gosein, is a [2]s __ __ g w __ __ t __ __. She has [3]w __ __ t __ __ __ lots of great songs. She writes the music and the [4]l __ __ i __ s. She has also been singing [5]s __ __ c __ the year 2000. Beyoncé, Shakira and Jordin Sparks are just three singers who have [6]s __ __ __ her songs.

PJ Harvey is a British singer and musician. She has an amazing [7]v __ __ __ e. She has been [8]p __ __ y __ __ __ music for over twenty-five years and she has [9]w __ __ many awards. Her albums, [10]w __ __ c __ are all brilliant, don't get to number one in the [11]c __ __ r __ s, but they all sell a lot of copies and usually get to about number ten.

.../10

4 Skills practice

SKILLS FOCUS: **READING, LISTENING** AND **WRITING**

Read

1 **Read the letter and write the names of the books and the authors.**

1 Animal Farm by ...

Dear Parents,

We are pleased to inform you that the Year 9 English Literature study books for next year will be *Animal Farm* and *Journey to the River Sea*.

We have chosen these books for a number of reasons. *Animal Farm* is an important book in the history of English literature. I'm sure many students have read it already. George Orwell, who wrote many important books, used the idea of animals taking over a farm to discuss the real world. Students can read and enjoy it as a simple story about animals. During the school year, they will learn about the message behind the story.

Journey to the River Sea, which is an exciting story that both boys and girls will enjoy, was written by Eva Ibbotson in 2001. It is set in 1910 and will give students useful historical information about that time. What's more, the story includes excellent descriptions of journeys and different countries, which will help students with their own writing.

We are sure that both you and your child will be happy with the choice of books. If you have any comments or questions, please contact me at the school.

Yours,

Connor Robertson

Head of English

2 **Choose the correct options.**

1 The letter is to parents of children **already in Year 9** / in Year 9 next year.
2 *Animal Farm* is **difficult** / **easy** to understand.
3 The students will learn more about **the real meaning of the book** / **the animals in the book**.
4 *Journey to the River Sea* was written in **2001** / **1910**.
5 *Journey to the River Sea* could be useful for **students' writing skills** / **students who want to travel**.
6 The writer of the letter **wants ideas for books for the students** / **is happy to explain why he has chosen these books**.

Listen

3 🎧 **Listen to an English teacher talking to a class and choose the correct options.**

1 Book this term: Framed / **Animal Farm**.
2 It was the author's **first** / **second** book.
3 The book is set in **Liverpool** / **Wales**.
4 The hero of the book is **Manod** / **Dylan**.

4 🎧 **Listen again and complete the information.**

Author: Frank Cottrell Boyce

1 Born: In Liverpool in *1959*.
2 Number of books written: _____
3 Number of awards won: _____
4 He wrote *Framed* in _____.
5 Dylan's parents own a _____.
6 Dylan follows some _____ which drive through the town.
7 The author got the idea from a story he read in a _____.

Write

5 **Rewrite the sentences using the linking words in brackets.**

1 We have to read a Shakespeare play and a book by Dickens this year. (as well as)

As well as reading a Shakespeare play, we have to read a book by Dickens this year.

2 These books are interesting and useful for our own writing. (not only ... but also)

_____

3 I've read all Shakespeare's plays and I've seen five of them at the theatre. (what's more)

_____

4 We're reading three books in English this year and learning how to write poetry. (as well as)

_____

6 **Write a review of a book which you have had to read for school.**

Vocabulary: Landscape and natural environment

1 ⭐ **Circle the odd-one-out.**

1 bush	tree	(river)
2 river	lake	desert
3 sea	hill	ocean
4 harbour	mountain	hill
5 island	valley	coast
6 field	waterfall	river

2 ⭐⭐ **Match the numbers on the map to the words in the box. There are three extra words.**

- cliffs [9]
- harbour [ ]
- desert [ ]
- forest [ ]
- ocean [ ]
- rocks [ ]
- coast [ ]
- path [ ]
- waterfall [ ]
- lake [ ]
- island [ ]
- hill [ ]

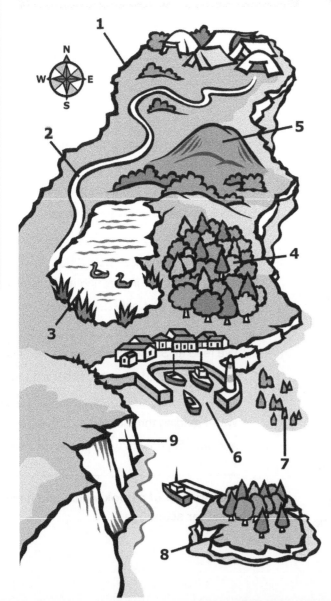

Grammar: First conditional with *if, unless, provided that, as long as*

3 ⭐ **Look at the information and choose the correct options.**

Welcome to Dreamworld

The resort that makes your dreams come true!

Open every day of the year*

*sometimes we need to close to clean the pools

Sundays: FREE
Wednesdays: No children day
Concerts: Every Saturday night

Free parking for guests (€20 a day for those without tickets)

1 a) We will be open every day of the year (**unless**) / **as long as** we have to clean the pools.

b) If we have to clean the pools, the resort **won't be** / **will be** open.

2 a) If you **come** / **will come** on Sundays, you won't have to pay.

b) You will have to pay **provided that** / **unless** you come on Sundays.

3 a) You can bring children to the resort **as long as** / **unless** you don't come on a Wednesday.

b) There **will be** / **won't be any** children in the resort unless you come on a Wednesday.

4 a) **Provided that** / **Unless** you stay until Saturday evening, you will be able to see one of our great concerts.

b) You won't see a concert if you **don't** / **won't** come to the resort on a Saturday.

5 a) You won't have to pay for the car park **provided that** / **unless** you have a ticket for the resort.

b) If you **don't** / **won't** have a ticket for the resort, you will have to pay €20 a day to park.

5 NATURAL WORLD

4 ★★★ **Complete the text with one word in each gap.**

Dear Janice,

You must go to Dreamworld. It's great, but quite expensive ¹*unless* you go on a Sunday. It's free on Sundays, but it's not too crowded ² _____ that you get there early. As ³ _____ as you arrive by nine o'clock and leave before midday, you can have a good time. If you go, make sure you phone first. It's open every day ⁴_____ that they don't have to clean the pools. We went once and found that it was closed, which was very annoying, but ⁵ _____ long ⁶_____ you phone or check on the internet, you'll be OK.

We're going next week ⁷_____ my dad has to work on Saturday. Why don't you come with us?

Love
Debbie

5 ★★★ **Make questions and answers from the prompts. Use the first conditional and the words in brackets.**

Island Survivor

Fifteen young people will live on an island for fourteen weeks. You choose who goes each week.

Your questions answered …

Q: ¹what/happen ⟹ they/get lost (if)
What will happen if they get lost?

A: ²they/not get lost ⟹ do/what they are told (provided that)
_____

Q: ³I/miss a show ⟹ I/be able/to see it later (if)
_____

A: ⁴you/be able to see it later ⟹ you/got the internet (as long as)
_____

Q: ⁵how much/it/cost ⟹ I/want to phone in (if)
_____

A: ⁶it/cost/5p a minute ⟹ you/use a mobile phone (unless)
_____

⁷you/use a mobile phone ⟹ it/cost/50p a minute (if)
_____

Grammar summary

First conditional with *if, unless, provided that, as long as*

Affirmative

If we **leave** now, we**'ll arrive** on time.
They**'ll have** a picnic on the beach **unless** it **rains**.
She**'ll let** us have a party **provided that** we **tidy up** after it.
I**'ll go** with you **as long as** the tickets **are** free.

Negative

If you **don't work** hard, you **won't get** a good mark in your exams.
I **won't help** you with your schoolwork **unless** you **try** to do it yourself first.
Provided that students **attend** all lessons, they **won't have** problems in the exams.
You **won't have** any problems with your exams **as long as** you **study** hard.

Questions	Short answers
Will it **be** a problem **if** we **have** a party?	Yes, it **will**. No, it **won't**.

Note

Use

- We use
  - the first conditional to talk about something that may happen in the future as a result of something else happening (or not happening).
  - *If it **rains**, I**'ll stay** at home.*
  - *if/provided that/as long as* for the result of an action happening.
    ***As long as** it doesn't finish too late, I'll go to the party.*
  - *unless* for the result of an action not happening.
    unless has a similar meaning to *if not*.
    *I won't go out **unless** I finish my homework.*

Form

- There are two parts in a first conditional sentence. We use *if/unless/provided that/as soon as* + present simple for the condition. We use *will* + infinitive without *to* for the result. We can write the two clauses in either order. If the condition clause is first, we separate the two clauses with a comma.
  *I**'ll go** climbing **if** there**'s** a guide with us.*
  *If there**'s** a guide with us, I**'ll go** climbing.*

Common mistakes

~~If it will be a nice day, I'll go for a walk.~~ ✗
*If it **is** a nice day, I'll go for a walk.* ✓
~~I will finish unless you help me.~~ ✗
*I **won't** finish unless you help me.* ✓

Vocabulary: Extreme weather and natural disasters

1 ⭐ **Find ten more extreme weather and natural disaster words.**

L	I	G	H	T	N	I	N	G	A
A	A	B	C	H	D	E	F	G	H
N	H	T	S	U	N	A	M	I	O
D	U	I	J	N	K	L	M	N	H
S	R	P	Q	D	R	S	T	S	A
L	R	U	V	E	W	G	X	T	I
I	I	T	O	R	N	A	D	O	L
D	C	Y	Z	A	B	L	C	R	S
E	A	D	E	I	G	E	F	M	T
J	N	K	N	H	L	O	M	P	O
H	E	A	T	W	A	V	E	S	R
Q	S	N	O	W	S	T	O	R	M

2 ⭐⭐ **Complete the headlines with extreme weather or natural disaster words.**

1
A_valanche_ **in France**
Snow from mountain destroys twenty houses

2 **B_____ in London**
Roads closed because of wind and snow

3 **D_____ in Australia**
There hasn't been rain here for two years

4 **F_____ in Bangladesh**
Thousands lose their homes as water levels rise two metres

5 **C_____ in the USA**
Houses and trees destroyed by 200 kmph winds

6 **E_____ in Greece**
Houses shook for five minutes; no serious injuries

7 **F_____ in Africa**
UN brings in food to help starving people

8 **V_____ e_____ in Japan**
People run to escape burning rocks thrown from the mountain

Grammar: Future time clauses with *when, until, as soon as, by the time, before*

3 ⭐ **Complete the email with the correct form of the verbs in brackets.**

To: All tornado chasers
From: Brad
Subject: Tornado

Hi Guys

The tornado should arrive tomorrow afternoon. Here's the plan.

Before the tornado [1]_arrives_ (arrive), we [2]_____ (prepare) our cameras and recording equipment.
As soon as we [3]_____ (see) the tornado, we [4]_____ (drive) towards it.
We [5]_____ (film) the storm when we [6]_____ (get) close to it.
You can't wait for the perfect shot. Tornadoes move fast and by the time your camera [7]_____ (be) ready, the tornado [8]_____ (not be) in the same place. Take as many photos as you can and there'll certainly be one or two good ones.
We [9]_____ (not leave) the area until the tornado [10]_____ (disappear), so eat before you leave home. Please don't bring food with you. The last time we got too close to a tornado in Kansas and our picnic ended up in Oklahoma!

Brad

4 Complete the messages with the words from the box. Put the verbs into the correct form.

- tell • by the time (x2) • not know
- as soon as (x2) • until (x2) • not be
- before • arrive

Rosy at 16.46 on 10 June wrote
Does anyone know anything about the voluntary work in the summer holidays yet?

Terri at 16.59 on 10 June wrote
Nothing. We ¹*won't know* anything ² _____ Kelly gets in touch. ³ _____ she emails me, I'll let you know.

Rosy at 17.06 on 10 June wrote
⁴ _____ Kelly emails, there ⁵ _____ any choice of jobs. We'll have to clean toilets or something!

Terri at 17.12 on 10 June wrote
Don't worry, I'm sure Kelly will write soon.

Kelly at 18.23 on 14 June wrote
Hi, Kelly here. I've found us work for three weeks in Wales.

Terri at 18.31 on 14 June wrote
Great! What kind of work?

Kelly at 18.43 on 14 June wrote
Well, it's on a farm, but we won't know exactly what we have to do ⁶ _____ the brochure ⁷ _____.

Rosy at 18.53 on 14 June wrote
Well, I hope it's OK. ⁸ _____ the brochure arrives, it'll be the summer holidays! I want to find out as much as I can about the place and the work ⁹ _____ we go.

Kelly at 19.05 on 14 June wrote
Stop worrying, Rosy. I'll probably get it tomorrow. ¹⁰ _____ it arrives, I ¹¹ _____ you all about it.

Grammar summary

Future time clauses with *when, until, as soon as, by the time, before*

I'll go out with my friends **when** I **finish** my exams.
As soon as/When we **hear** the bell, we'll leave the room.
We won't ring you **until** we **arrive**.
By the time John **arrives**, the film will be over.
I'll finish my homework **before** I **watch** TV.

Note

Use
- We use *will* future with *when, until, as soon as, by the time, before* to show that
  - something will happen at a specific time in the future.
  - two future events will happen at almost the same time or one immediately after the other.
  - one thing will happen very quickly after the other.
  I'll talk to you when I arrive.
  By the time you get this, I'll be in Manchester.
  As soon as we find a hotel, we'll phone you.

Form
- There are two parts in a future time clause. We use *will* + infinitive without *to* for the result. We use *when, until, as soon as, by the time, before* + present simple for what happens first. If the *when, until, as soon as, by the time, before* clause is first, we use a comma.
  I'll decide what to do before I go to the meeting.
  As soon as we're ready, we'll leave.
- The *will* clause can be affirmative or negative, the *when, until, as soon as, by the time, before* clause is usually affirmative.
  We won't know our exam results before we go on holiday.
- We don't usually use *until* at the start of a sentence.
  I won't stop reading until my mum tells me to go to sleep.

Common mistakes
~~When I will see you, I'll tell you what happened.~~ ✗
When I **see** you, I'll tell you what happened.✓
~~I was cycling while it started raining.~~ ✗
I was cycling **when** it started raining. ✓

5c In case it gets cold ...

Phrases

1 ✦ **Choose the correct options.**

1 Adrian: What are you **after** / **over** /
up to?

   Tim: Some camping equipment
for my holiday in the
mountains.

2 Adrian: Are you going to buy those
walking boots?

   Tim: I'd love to, but I've only
got a fiver **to** / **on** / **for** me.

3 Tim: I'm interested in this
camping stove, but it's in
its box and I can't see it
properly.

Assistant: I'll open it **out** / **off** / **up** for
you if you like.

4 Tim: Neil doesn't want to come
camping with us because
he can't live without a TV
for two weeks.

Adrian: How **poor** / **sad** / **lonely** is
that!

Grammar: *in case* + present simple

2 ✦ **Complete the dialogue with the present simple form of the verbs in brackets.**

Joe: Right, Mum, I'm all
packed and ready to go
to Greece. Ben and his
parents will be here in a
minute. ... What's that?

Mum: Just a few things you
might need. An
umbrella, in case it
¹*rains* (rain). A blanket in
case you ² _____ (be) cold at night. A CD player
in case your MP3 player ³ _____ (not work).
Some books in case you ⁴ _____ (not have)
anything to do in the evenings. A cookbook in case you
⁵ _____ (not like) Greek food. Some batteries in
case the shops ⁶ _____ (not sell) them. A Greek
dictionary in case the people ⁷ _____ (not speak)
English ...

Joe: ... and some money for a doctor in case I hurt my back
with this heavy rucksack! It won't rain, it won't be cold
and I've got everything I need in here!

3 ✦✦ **Read the chat then rewrite the sentences using *in case* and the present simple.**

Beth > Are you all ready for the concert tomorrow night?

Angie > ¹Yes. I'm going to do all my homework tonight
because I might be too tired on Sunday.

Beth > ²Me too. I'm going to read my English notes too
because Mr Davies might give us a surprise test on
Monday.

Angie > ³I'm going to get my tickets on the internet tonight
because there might be a long queue tomorrow.

Beth > Good idea. What about money? How much are you
going to take?

Angie > ⁴I'm going to take some money for a taxi because
we might miss the last bus.

Beth > What about money for food?

Angie > ⁵I'm going to take sandwiches because there might
not be any food there.

Beth > Do you think we'll meet Robbie?

Angie > I don't know. I think ⁶I'll take a CD because he might
come out to sign autographs after the concert.

B: Are you all ready for the concert tomorrow
night?

A: ¹Yes. I'm going to do all my homework tonight
in case I'm too tired on Sunday.

B: ²I'm going to read my English notes too _____
_____.

A: ³I'm going to get my tickets on the internet
tonight _____.

B: Good idea. What about money? How much are
you going to take?

A: ⁴I'm going to take money for a taxi _____
_____.

B: What about money for food?

A: ⁵I'm going to take sandwiches _____
_____.

B: Do you think we'll meet Robbie?

A: I don't know. ⁶I think I'll take a CD _____
_____.

Vocabulary: Camping equipment

4 ⭐ **Look at the pictures and complete the words.**

Things to take

Sleeping and other things

A ¹<u>tent</u>, a good ²s_____

b_____ to keep me warm, a strong

³r_____ to carry everything in and a

⁴t_____ for the nighttime.

Food

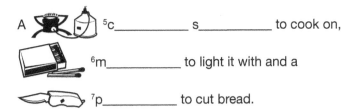

A ⁵c_____ s_____ to cook on,

⁶m_____ to light it with and a

⁷p_____ to cut bread.

Problems

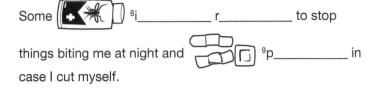

Some ⁸i_____ r_____ to stop

things biting me at night and ⁹p_____ in

case I cut myself.

Use your English: Make and respond to requests

5 ⭐ **Choose the correct options.**

Tom: Could I ¹**borrow** / **lend** / **give** £10 from you? I want to buy a penknife and a torch.

Leo: ²**True** / **Sure** / **Really**, here you are.

Tom: That's brilliant. I'll ³**lend** / **borrow** / **give** it back tomorrow.

Steve: Would you mind ⁴**lend** / **to lend** / **lending** me £5?

Kate: I'm ⁵**sorry** / **sad** / **upset**, I can't. I haven't got £5.

Steve: ⁶**Don't** / **Never** / **Nothing** mind.

Ray: Could you ⁷**take** / **get** / **borrow** me some insect repellent from the shops?

Liam: Yes, of ⁸**sure** / **fine** / **course**.

Ray: Thanks. I'll ⁹**do** / **make** / **have** the same for you one day.

Natalie: Could you ¹⁰**borrow** / **take** / **lend** me your homework? I haven't done it.

Cathy: I'd ¹¹**think** / **rather** / **like** not if you don't mind. I don't like people copying my homework.

Natalie: OK. It doesn't ¹²**mind** / **matter** / **worry**. I'll ask Amelia.

Grammar summary

in case + present simple

Take your mobile phone with you **in case** you **want** to call us later.

Tom always has two alarm clocks on in the morning **in case** one **doesn't work**.

Note

Use

- We use *in case* + present simple to say what we do now because something bad might happen later.

  *I've got some sandwiches **in case** I **get** hungry later on.*

Common mistakes

~~Finish your homework now in case you will want to go out later.~~ ✗

*Finish your homework now in case you **want** to go out later.* ✓

5 Language round-up

1 Complete the email with the words from the box. Put the verbs into the correct form.

- hill • not go • lake • if • provided • sleep
- unless • have to • ~~island~~ • do • long

Hi Sara,
Thanks for the email about the rock festival in the park. It sounds great, but are you sure that the bands play on the ¹*island* in the middle of the ²_____? How will they get all their sound equipment there?
Do you really want to camp on Saturday night? I don't mind staying in a tent, but I ³_____ camping ⁴_____ there are proper toilets! I'm worried about the weather too. What ⁵_____ we _____ if it rains? I ⁶_____ in the tent ⁷_____ that it's warm and dry. If it rains, I think we should go home for the night. It's not far and my dad will come for us ⁸_____ we want.
One last question. If we go, ⁹_____ we _____ buy tickets or is it free? I can pay for a ticket as ¹⁰_____ as they aren't too expensive. If they're expensive, there's a ¹¹_____ near the park. We could climb that and watch from the top!
Write soon,
Meg

.../10

2 Match the beginnings (1–11) to the correct endings (a–k).

1 I'll go to bed as soon
2 I'll be too tired to dance by the
3 I can't light this camping
4 I'll have a party unless
5 You'll be fine, provided
6 Oh no! I forgot the insect
7 I've got a torch in
8 If everyone turns up, it will
9 We can't have tuna without a tin
10 I'll have a party if
11 I won't decide about the holidays until

a) repellent.
b) that you're careful.
c) my mum says 'Yes'.
d) as I get home.
e) be great!
f) opener.
g) time the concert starts.
h) school finishes.
i) my mum says 'No'.
j) case it's dark.
k) stove.

.../10

3 Choose the correct words and rearrange the letters to form words for extreme weather or natural disasters.

- We want to go to Ireland, but we won't go ¹ until / **by the time** the ²*flood* (ldofo) water disappears.
- We're going camping in France in August. There's a ³_____ (aeatvehw) there at the moment, but I know that ⁴until / **as soon as** Dad starts putting the tent up, there'll be a sudden ⁵_____ (hmertdorntus)!
- We're going to the Alps next week, but there was an ⁶_____ (nvclahaea) there last week and they won't open the ski slopes ⁷**when** / **until** they're safe.
- We're going to Italy in August. There was an ⁸_____ (hakuareqet) there last November, but, ⁹**as soon as** / **by the time** we get there, everything will be normal again.
- We'll either go to Florida in July, ¹⁰**until** / **before** the ¹¹_____ (ruieahrnc) season starts or in December after it ¹²**will finish** / **finishes**.

.../10

4 Complete the text with the correct form of the words in brackets or one word in each gap.

You're going to a music festival. But what ¹*will you do* (you/do) if it ²_____ (rain)? You'll be worried ³_____ you've got a TENT COAT! You can wear it as a coat, but, as ⁴_____ as the music ⁵_____ (finish), you can simply lie down in your own tent!
You might also want to take some food, in ⁶_____ you get hungry – by the ⁷_____ you find the hot dog stall, your favourite band ⁸_____ (be) on stage! Well, you don't have to worry as ⁹_____ as you've got a MAGIC MEAL. If you've got a MAGIC MEAL, you ¹⁰_____ (not be) hungry and you ¹¹_____ (not miss) your favourite band!

.../10

LISTEN AND CHECK YOUR SCORE

Total	.../40

5 Skills practice

SKILLS FOCUS: READING AND **WRITING**

Read

1 **Read and complete the text with the sentences (A–C).**

A Quite a lot of people were hurt.

B In all that time, there had never been an accident before.

C The sea here is home to seals and whales.

Arctic Cruises are becoming more and more popular. Because of global warming, there isn't much ice and it is easier for boats to sail. One popular place to visit is the Svalbard Islands, in Norway. ¹___ However, most people want to see the polar bears that live on the islands.

In 2007, fifty tourists were travelling on a boat, the *Alexey Maryshev*. They were looking at the glacier above their heads. Suddenly, a large piece of ice broke off and crashed down into the sea. There was a huge wave and pieces of ice went everywhere. The ship started rolling because of the wave and people fell over on the deck. ²___ Doctors treated some of the injured people on the boat and a helicopter took three people to hospital in Tromsø, Norway. Luckily, the boat was not damaged and sailed back to the capital of the islands, Longyearbyen.

The tour was organised by the British tour company Discover the World. It has been organising trips to the Arctic for twenty years. ³___ A spokesperson said that the tourists on the boat were looking for adventure and excitement. They certainly got that!

2 **Read the text again and decide whether the sentences are true (T), false (F) or it doesn't say (DS).**

1 It is easier to sail to the Arctic now because there is less ice in the sea. `T`

2 Polar bears are the only animals that live in the Svalbard Islands. ☐

3 When the ice crashed into the sea, fifty people were standing on the boat's deck. ☐

4 We don't know exactly how many people were hurt in the accident. ☐

5 It wasn't the first time that a Discover the World tour had had an accident. ☐

Write

3 **Complete the factfile with the information from the box.**

- Norwegian • 61,022 km² • Longyearbyen
- ~~500 km north of Norway~~ • 2,321
- polar bears, reindeer, arctic foxes

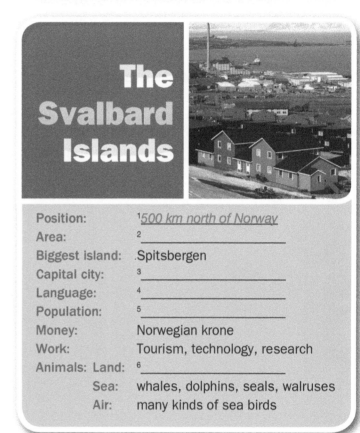

The Svalbard Islands

Position:	¹*500 km north of Norway*
Area:	²_____
Biggest island:	.Spitsbergen
Capital city:	³_____
Language:	⁴_____
Population:	⁵_____
Money:	Norwegian krone
Work:	Tourism, technology, research
Animals: Land:	⁶_____
Sea:	whales, dolphins, seals, walruses
Air:	many kinds of sea birds

4 **Use the information in Exercise 3 to write a fact sheet about the Svalbard Islands. Use these headings and ideas:**

Where are the islands and how big are they?
Names of islands, area, position

Who lives there and what do they do?
Population, nationality, work

What animals can you see there?
Land, sea and air

Svalbard Islands Fact Sheet
Where are the islands and how big are they?
The Svalbard Islands are a group of islands ...

6a If you were invisible for a day, ...

Grammar: Second conditional with *would, might, could*

1 ⭐ **Complete the text with the second conditional form of the verbs in brackets.**

http://www.friendsfound.co.uk

FRIENDS ◇ FOUND   Home   Profile   Friends   Inbox

WHAT WOULD YOU DO?

COMPARE YOUR IDEAS WITH YOUR FRIENDS!

Where [1]*would you travel* (you/travel) to if you [2]_____ (have) a time machine?
If you [3]_____ (want) to meet a famous person, you [4]_____ (can go) back in time or you [5]_____ (may prefer) to see what the future looks like. It's your choice! If time travel [6]_____ (be) possible, you [7]_____ (may like) to see someone famous in concert like The Beatles or Elvis. Which band would you want to see? You might not want to travel in time. If you [8]_____ (can see) any band you wanted, you [9]_____ (may choose) to get a ticket to see your favourite band playing now. Or here's another idea. If you [10]_____ (travel) to the future, you [11]_____ (can find out) who will be popular next year. You [12]_____ (can tell) all your friends about this brilliant band you know. They'd be amazed next year when the band you told them about became superstars!

2 ⭐⭐ **Complete the texts with the correct form of the verbs from the box.**

• can manage • make • practise • become • tell • choose • know
• may become • ~~can play~~ • join

http://www.friendsfound.co.uk

FRIENDS ◇ FOUND   Home   Profile   Friends   Inbox

IF YOU COULD HAVE ONE ABILITY, WHAT ABILITY WOULD YOU CHOOSE?   COMMENTS (2)

Matt wrote: I'd like to be able to play the guitar. If I [1]*could play* the guitar, I [2]_____ a band. If we [3]_____ a lot, we [4]_____ famous. If we [5]_____ famous, we [6]_____ lots of money.

Steve wrote: OK, Matt, so if you were in a band, I [7]_____ the ability to make money and to be a good businessman. If I [8]_____ how to make money, I [9]_____ your band. I'm sure I'd be a good manager!

Matt wrote: Hmm, I don't know. If you were our manager, you [10]_____ us what to do. I don't think I'd like that!

6 IMAGINATION

44

Vocabulary: Transitive phrasal verbs

3 🔲 **Tick (✓) the correct sentences and cross (X) the incorrect sentences.**

1 a) Let's check out the new sports shop. ✓

   b) Let's check the new sports shop out. ✓

   c) Let's check it out. ✓

   d) Let's check out it. X

2 a) Pick that rubbish up. ☐

   b) Pick up that rubbish. ☐

   c) Pick it up. ☐

   d) Pick up it. ☐

3 a) We should switch off the TV now. ☐

   b) We should switch it off now. ☐

   c) We should switch off it now. ☐

   d) We should switch the TV off now. ☐

4 a) Can you give me back my book, please? ☐

   b) Can you give back me my book, please? ☐

   c) Can you give me my book back, please? ☐

   d) Can you give me it back, please? ☐

4 🔲 **Complete the sentences with one word from each box. Put the verbs into the correct form. There are two extra words in each box.**

• put   • take
• find   • check
• pick   • ~~turn~~
• switch   • turn

• out   • up   • on
• ~~off~~   • up   • off
• out   • in

1 Are you watching TV again? _Turn_ it _off_ and go outside for some fresh air.

2 Did you _____ _____ what Joe was up to last night?

3 I _____ _____ that new computer shop yesterday. It's good. They sell lots of games.

4 Can you _____ _____ the radio? I like this show, but I can't hear it at the moment.

5 Quick! _____ _____ Channel 9 news. There's a story about our school.

6 We tidied the school playground yesterday. I _____ _____ twenty-seven crisp packets!

Grammar summary

Second conditional with *would, might, could*

Affirmative

If I **had** more money, I **would pay** for your pizza.

If Tom **worked** harder, he **might do** better in his exams.

If I **understood** French, I **could translate** this letter for you.

Negative

If I **lived** nearer my school, I **wouldn't have to** get up so early.

If Sara had a computer, she **might not go out** so often.

You **couldn't phone** me if you **didn't have** my number.

Questions

What **would** you **say** if Natalie **asked** you **out**?

If you **were** me, what **would** you **do**?

Note

Use

• We use the second conditional to talk about unreal or unlikely situations in the present or future.

   *If I **had** a million dollars, I **could buy** an island.*

Form

• There are two parts in a second conditional sentence. We use *if* + past simple for the unreal or unlikely condition. We use *would, might, could* + infinitive without *to* for the result.

   *If you **were** more careful, you **might not lose** your phone so often.*

• We can write the two clauses in either order. When the *if* (condition) clause is first, we separate the two clauses with a comma.

   *If we **were** older, I **would ask** you to marry me.*

   *I **would ask** you to marry me if we **were** older.*

***be* in the second conditional**

• In informal written or spoken language, we say *If I/he/she/it **was** ... .*

   *If I **was** better at football, I could be in the school team.*

• In formal written or spoken language, we say *If I/he/she/it **were** ... .*

   *If I **were** you, I'd use a different search engine.*

6b If only I had my camera!

Phrases

1 ⭐ Complete the dialogues with one word in each gap.

8.05 p.m.

Rob: OK. I got two DVDs for six pounds. So, that's two pounds each for you, me and Annie.

Callum: ¹T*hat's* ²a_____ very ³w_____, but we only agreed to get one DVD. I have to be home by 10.30 p.m. I won't be able to watch both of them.

Annie: Me too. We'll give you a pound each, Rob, not two pounds!

8.35 p.m.

Callum: Rob, before we watch the film, let's get a pizza.

Rob: Not for me, thanks. I'm not hungry.

Callum: OK. Come on Annie. ⁴S_____ you ⁵i_____ a few minutes, Rob.

8.55 p.m.

Rob: Mmm, that pizza smells nice.

Callum: ⁶H_____ ⁷o_____! This is mine. I'm starving.

Grammar: *wish/if only* + past simple

2 ⭐ Make sentences from the prompts and match them to the people in the pictures.

1 wish/be/at the beach

   I wish I was at the beach. [D]

2 only/can/play the guitar

   _____ ☐

3 wish/not be/so tired

   _____ ☐

4 only/know/what he/is/talking about

   _____ ☐

5 wish/have/a time machine

   _____ ☐

6 only/not have to/wear this uniform

   _____ ☐

3 ⭐ Write sentences with *I wish* or *If only* and the past simple.

Things wrong with my life

Appearance:	¹too short
Personality:	²too shy
Possessions:	³no MP3 player
	⁴really old computer
Abilities:	⁵not very good at singing
Friends:	⁶don't know many people here
	⁷have to come home very early in the evening
School work:	⁸always get poor marks
	⁹my mum worries about me all the time

... but Maria emailed today and she wants to meet on Saturday! Maybe there's nothing wrong with my life after all. 😊

1 I *wish I was* taller.

2 If _____ so shy.

3 I _____ an MP3 player.

4 If _____ so old.

5 I _____ sing better.

6 If _____ more people here.

7 I _____ to come home so early in the evening.

8 If _____ better marks at school.

9 I _____ about me so much.

Use your English: Ask for and give advice

4 ⭐ **Complete the messages with one word in each gap.**

I'm having a party and I'm going to invite most of the people in my class. There's one girl that I don't want to invite, but I'm worried that she'll be upset. What do you think I ¹s<u>hould</u> do? *Vicky*

Why ²d_____ you tell her that it's just a small party and you can only invite a few people. *Andy*

I'm not ³s_____ that's a good idea. There might be photos of the party on the internet. She might see them. If I ⁴w_____ you, I wouldn't say anything. *Cathy*

---

⁵M_____ you're right. I don't want to lie to her. *Vicky*

I think my boyfriend is seeing someone else. He's always too busy to see me. What ⁶w_____ you do if you were me? *Eva*

Have you ⁷t_____ asking him? *Max*

You should wait outside his house and follow him to see where he goes and who he sees. *Tim*

That's a bit ⁸o_____ the top! *Jess*

I don't think that ⁹s_____ a very sensible idea. He might see me. *Eva*.

Grammar summary

wish/if only + past simple

Affirmative

I **wish/If only** I **was/were** taller.
I **wish/If only** we **had** more money.
I **wish/If only** I **could** play the piano.

Negative

I **wish/If only** I **wasn't/weren't** so short.
I **wish/If only** I **didn't love** her so much.
I **wish/If only** my little brother **couldn't open** my bedroom door!

Note

Use

- We use this verb pattern to talk about present wishes or regrets when the present wish or regret is unlikely or impossible.
  *I **wish** I **could** play the guitar.*
  ***If only** we **had** more time.*

Form

- We use the past simple with *I wish* or *If only* to talk about a situation now or in the future.
  *I **wish** I **had** some money.* (now)
  *I **wish** I **could** go on holiday with you.* (this summer)

Common mistakes

~~*I wish I have a motorbike.*~~ ✗
*I wish I **had** a motorbike.* ✓
~~*If only I can speak Italian.*~~ ✗
*If only I **could** speak Italian.* ✓

6c We didn't mind queuing.

1 ⭐ Complete the text with the infinitive or gerund form of the verbs in brackets.

It's the great switch off!

Are we all addicted to computers? Can we survive without them? We asked one family to switch off their computers for a week. The Collins family from Durham agreed ¹*to try* (try). Mr Collins hoped ²_____ (have) more time to decorate the house. Mrs Collins didn't mind ³_____ (not use) the computer because she only uses it to email friends. She has often tried ⁴_____ (stop) her daughter playing computer games, but without success. Fifteen-year-old Laura admitted ⁵_____ (spend) a lot of time on the computer, but denied ⁶_____ (be) worried about not having one for a week.

So the question was … would the family manage ⁷_____ (survive) for a whole week without their computers? As the week approached, they seemed ⁸_____ (be) quite excited by the idea …

One week later, we visited the Collins family again.

Did they survive? Mr and Mrs Collins had enjoyed ⁹_____ (do) other things. Laura found it more of a problem. At first she practised ¹⁰_____ (play) the guitar, but she soon got bored. When we suggested ¹¹_____ (continue) the experiment for a second week, she locked herself in her bedroom … with her computer on.

2 ⭐⭐ Complete the text with the infinitive or gerund form of the verbs from the box.

• ~~visit~~ • do • think • start • be • walk • go • wait (x2) • try • look

ART ATTACK

A few years ago, my parents wanted ¹*to visit* as many museums and art galleries as they could. I love ²_____ at paintings, but everywhere was so crowded. No one enjoys ³_____ for hours to get in and I can't stand ⁴_____ round big cities in very hot weather. In the end, we gave up ⁵_____ to get into museums and spent most of our time in parks. So, Dad suggested ⁶_____ the same thing, but in the winter holidays. We decided ⁷_____ with Rome. I expected it ⁸_____ crowded, but it was beautifully quiet. The following year, we all agreed ⁹_____ to Paris. I had never seen the Mona Lisa because I had refused ¹⁰_____ in the queues outside the Louvre. This time, as we walked to the gallery, I kept ¹¹_____ 'It must be closed. There's no one here.' But it wasn't! Next February, we're going to Florence.

Vocabulary: Noun suffixes -ion, -ment, -ity and -y

3 🔹 **Make nouns with the endings given using the verbs from the box.**

> • difficult • coordinate • move • accurate
> • real • organise • ~~able~~ • improve

-ion: _____, _____

-ment: _____, _____

-ity: *ability*, _____

-y: _____, _____

4 🔹 **Complete the text with the noun form of the words in brackets.**

The London observatory and planetarium in Greenwich is a great museum. We made the ¹*decision* (decide) to go there because you can be half in the east

of the world and half in the west. There was no ² _____ (difficult) finding it because it's on a hill in a park.

We went in and paid for our tickets and then decided to get a photo of us on the east/west line. There was a long queue, but it was fun watching the ³ _____ (excite) on the faces of the people at the front. There was a nice spirit of ⁴ _____ (cooperate) too, as people took each other's photos.

After we had taken the photos, we looked round the museum. It was a bit of a ⁵ _____ (disappoint) to be honest, but it was OK.

We then saw a film in the planetarium. It was called 'A ⁶ _____ (discover) of the stars.' It was a mixture of education and ⁷ _____ (entertain). I enjoyed it a lot. It encouraged us to use our ⁸ _____ (imagine) and to think about the ⁹ _____ (possible) of finding life on other planets. I love films in planetariums – looking at the stars above your head. It's strange coming back to ¹⁰ _____ (real) when it's over. I couldn't believe it was still daylight outside! Overall, it was a good day out.

Grammar summary

Verb with infinitive or gerund
Verb with infinitive
I **want to go** out.
Mark has **decided to study** German.
They really **tried not to laugh**.
Verb with gerund
Lisa **can't stand being** late.
We **fancy having** pizza this evening.
Paolo **doesn't mind not getting** the bus.
Verb with infinitive or gerund
I've **started to learn/learning** French.
We **like to go/going** into town on Saturdays.

Note

Use

- We use the infinitive after some verbs, e.g. *agree, decide, encourage, expect, forget, help, hope, manage, offer, promise, refuse, seem, try, want, would like.*
  We **managed to get** to school on time.

- We use the gerund (*-ing* form) after some verbs, e.g. *admit, avoid, can't stand, carry on, deny, enjoy, fancy, finish, give up, keep, miss, not mind, practise, stop, suggest.*
  Stephen **denied using** his computer after his bedtime.

- We can use the gerund or infinitive after some verbs with little or no change in meaning, e.g. *hate, like, love, prefer, start.*
  We **started to get** ready.
  We **started getting** ready.

- Some verbs can be followed by an object before the infinitive.
  My mum **encouraged me to play** tennis.

Form

- In negative sentences, we add *not* before the gerund or the infinitive.
  I **promised not to be** late again.
  She **doesn't mind not having** a phone.

Common mistakes

~~I tried to not make any mistakes.~~ ✗
I tried **not to make** any mistakes. ✓

6 Language round-up

1 **Complete the dialogue with the correct form of the words from the box.**

> • only • might • could • if • ~~out~~
> • wouldn't • check • I'd • find • not have
> • talk • say

Nick: There's Lisa again. She's so cool. Why don't you ask her ¹_out_?

Dan: I'm still thinking about Amy. If ²_____ we were still together.

Nick: Amy! She's history! ³_____ you asked Lisa out, you would forget Amy.

Dan: If I ⁴_____ to Amy, she ⁵_____ go out with me again.

Nick: No, she ⁶_____. Amy's with Conrad now. Forget Amy. Lisa's really nice. If I ⁷_____ a girlfriend, ⁸_____ ask her out. Why don't you ⁹_____ out if she's busy at the weekend?

Dan: Where ¹⁰_____ I take her if she ¹¹_____ yes?

Nick: Well, you could ¹²_____ out the new café in the shopping mall …

.../11

2 **Make full sentences from the prompts.**

1A If only/we have/more money
   If only we had more money.

1B If/we have/more money/we can/go on holiday together

   _____

2A I wish/I can/speak French

   _____

2B If I can/speak French/I/talk/to Giselle

   _____

3A I wish/the DJ have/some better music

   _____

3B I dance/if the music/not be/so bad

   _____

.../10

3 **Complete the news stories with the correct form of the words in capitals.**

1 EXCITE / LEAVE / REAL
  Excitement on _Reality_ TV show as contestant refuses _to leave_!

2 DISAPPOINT / GIVE / BE / TRAVEL
  Do you wish you _____ somewhere else? Would you like _____ around the world? We have decided _____ away ten _free_ tickets. Enter _now_ to avoid _____.

3 BRAVE / LOOK / PLAY / BE
  The England captain showed great _____ in last night's match as he carried on _____ after losing two teeth. If only all our players _____ as brave. After the match, he said, 'I don't mind _____ strange, but I don't know what my wife is going to say when I get home!'

.../12

4 **Choose the correct options.**

1 What would you do if you ___ the lottery?
  a) won   b) win   c) would win

2 The music's too loud. Turn ___.
  a) down   b) them down   c) it down

3 I wish I ___ the answers to the French test.
  a) know   b) would know   c) knew

4 Your advice was a bit over the ___.
  a) edge   b) top   c) limit

5 Did you manage ___ your computer?
  a) to fix   b) fixing   c) fix

6 You have to use your ___ to write poetry.
  a) imagine   b) imagination   c) imagery

7 If only it ___ the holidays now.
  a) is   b) would be   c) was

8 I keep ___ stupid mistakes.
  a) to make   b) making   c) make

.../7

🎧 LISTEN AND CHECK YOUR SCORE	
Total	.../40

6 Skills practice

SKILLS FOCUS: READING, LISTENING AND **WRITING**

Read

1 **Match the headings (1–4) to the correct texts (A–C). There is one extra heading.**

1 On the big day. ☐   3 Finding a partner. ☐
2 What's wrong? ☐   4 Looking good! ☐

A

Every year, our school puts on an end-of-year disco. Every year, fewer people turn up. Every year, it is less and less interesting. It's not the music, it's not the school hall, it's just … nothing special. Let's do something else this year!

B

Why don't we organise a US-style 'end-of-year prom' this year? We've all seen them in films. People really try hard to look good. They think about their clothes for months before the prom. The girls look very glamorous in long dresses. The boys look like real gentlemen in black suits.

C

On the evening of the ball, the school will be like Hollywood. We'll have a red carpet outside the front of the school. At the prom, there will be a live band and a mixture of music so that people have to learn 'real' dancing, not just disco dancing!

I'm sure people would love the idea and it wouldn't cost the school much. Please sign my petition if you agree with me.

Debbie Fisher, Class 11D

2 **Read the text again and answer the questions.**

1 What does the school organise at the end of the year?   *a disco*

2 Where have students seen what proms are like?   _____

3 What clothes look glamorous on girls?
                    _____

4 What will the red carpet and other things make the school look like?   _____

Listen

3 🎧 Match the speakers (1–3) with the topics (a–c).

Speaker 1   a) I prefer the old style parties.

Speaker 2   b) Someone to go with.

Speaker 3   c) What to wear?

4 🎧 Listen again and complete the sentences.

Speaker 1

1 The Prom is in _____ months' time.

2 The boy she likes is tall and _____ and he can _____.

Speaker 2

3 Girls can choose the length, _____ and _____ of their dresses.

4 He might not be allowed into the ball if he wears jeans and a _____.

Speaker 3

5 He doesn't want to look _____ at a party because he wears a _____ every day.

6 At the old school discos, no one worried about what they _____.

Write

5 **You are organising a prom at school. Write an informal letter to your cousin in the USA. Use the plan below to help you.**

Paragraph 1: Start your letter

Greet your cousin

Ask how he/she is

Tell him/her your news

Paragraph 2: Explain why you are writing

Your idea for a prom

The reasons you think it's a good idea

Ask him/her about food, decoration and speeches

Paragraph 3: End the letter

Thank your cousin

Say goodbye

Give best wishes

7a He asked me if I had a website.

Phrases

1 Complete the dialogue with phrases from the box. There is one extra phrase.

> • quid • ~~Let me guess~~ • Well • actually • Can you call me • Thanks for calling back

Greg: Oh, Mr Davies. There was something I had to tell you … er …

Mr Davies: ¹*Let me guess*. Someone phoned and you've lost the message.

Greg: Not lost. I wrote her name down somewhere.

Mr Davies: How much do I pay you to take messages for me?

Greg: Fifty ²_____ a week.

Mr Davies: That's about forty-nine pounds too much.

Greg: Here it is. It was Natalie Glover who phoned.

Mr Davies: Oh good. Pass me the phone. … Natalie, hi. Colin Davies here.

Natalie: Colin! Hi! ³_____. I was a bit worried you wouldn't get my message. The boy who answered the phone sounded a bit confused.

Mr Davies: ⁴_____, ⁵_____ I nearly didn't get it. Greg's not the best worker. Anyway, let's not worry about him. What did you ring about?

Grammar: Reported statements and questions

2 Complete the sentences with the correct form of the verbs in brackets.

> My name is Tony Stark.

1 He said that his name *was* (be) Tony Stark.

> People think you are dead. Better you stay that way.

2 Tonto told John Reid that people _____ (think) that he _____ (be) dead and that it was better that he (stay) _____ that way.

> Animals have souls … I have seen it in their eyes.

3 Pi said that animals _____ (have) souls. He _____ (see) it in their eyes.

> I'm looking for someone to share in an adventure.

4 Gandalf said that he _____ (look) for someone to share in an adventure.

> Captain, can you get us to Bagghar?

5 Tintin asked Captain Haddock if he _____ (can) get them to Bagghar.

3 Complete the sentences with direct or reported speech.

1 **Mark:** 'I don't understand my homework.'
Mark said *that he didn't understand his homework*.

2 **Lisa:** 'I wasn't late last night.'
Lisa said _____
_____ .

3 **Nick:** '_____ ,'
Nick asked Dean if he wanted to play tennis.

4 **Jake:** '_____ ,'
Jake said that he had never seen that game before.

5 **Erin:** 'Has Dan got my MP3 player?'
Erin asked _____
_____ .

6 **Fiona:** 'Who ate my sandwiches?'
Fiona asked _____
_____ .

7 **Angie:** '_____ ,'
Angie asked if I could look at her laptop.

8 **Bill:** 'I'm not going out tonight.'
Bill said that _____
_____ .

Use your English: Phone messages

4 Complete the words with one letter in each gap.

Answer machine: Hello, you're [1]t h r o u g h to Beth Davies. I'm sorry, I'm not [2]a _ _ u _ d to answer the phone at the moment. Please [3]l _ _ _ e a message after the [4]t _ _ e and I'll get back to you.

Meg: Hello, Beth. This is Meg. I was just calling for a [5]c _ _ t. Can you [6]c _ _ l me when you get this [7]m _ s _ _ _ e?

Answer machine: Hello. This is Meg. I'm [8]a _ _ _ id I can't take your call, but leave a message and I'll get [9]b _ _ k to you.

Beth: Oh no! Hi, it's Beth. I got your message. I'll have my phone on all evening so [10]g _ _ e me a ring soon.

Grammar summary

Reported statements and questions

Direct statement	Reported statement
'I **play** computer games every day.'	He said (that) he **played** computer games every day.
'I**'m texting** my friend.'	Mick said (that) he **was texting** his friend.
'We **went** to the cinema last night.'	They said (that) they **had been** to the cinema the previous night.

Reported questions

Wh- questions

Direct question	Reported question
'Where **are** you **going**?'	He asked me where I **was going**.
'When **will** you **be** ready?'	She asked him when he **would be** ready.

Yes/No questions

Direct question	Reported question
'**Can** Steve **swim**?'	She asked us **if/whether** Steve **could** swim.
'**Will** you **tell** her?'	He asked me **if/whether** I **would tell** her.

Note
Form
- When we change a direct statement/question to a reported one, we make some changes to the structure.
  - We move the tense 'back'.
    'I **don't know** the answer.'
    'He said he **didn't know** the answer.'
  - We change pronouns and possessive adjectives where necessary.
    'I can't find **my** camera.'
    Dave said that **he** couldn't find **his** camera.
  - We change time and place references.
    'I saw Tom **yesterday**.'
    She said that she had seen Tom **the previous day**.
- If we are reporting something immediate, we don't need to change the tense or other words.
  It's Tim on the phone. He **says** he**'ll meet** us at 6 p.m.
- In reported *Wh-* questions, we use:
  asked + (object) + question word + subject + verb.
  Where do you live?
  He **asked me where I lived**.
- In reported *Yes/No* questions, we use:
  asked + (object) + if/whether + subject + verb.
  Have you got an invitation?
  They asked me **if I had got** an invitation.

7b You suggested getting a taxi.

Grammar: Reported speech with verbs of reporting

1 Match the sentences (1–8) to the verbs (a–j). There are two extra verbs.

1 Can you help me with this homework?
2 Would you like to come to my party?
3 This burger is disgusting. It's cold and hard.
4 I can help you tidy up if you want.
5 I'm not wearing that shirt!
6 Yes, it's true. I copied my homework from the internet.
7 I didn't write anything on the school wall.
8 I'm sorry I forgot your birthday.

a) admit
b) apologise
c) ask
d) complain
e) deny
f) explain
g) invite
h) keep
i) offer
j) refuse

2 Make reported sentences from the prompts.

'I'll be home by 9 p.m.' said Darren.

1 (Darren/promise) _Darren promised to be home by 9 p.m._

Darren met his friends. 'Hey, let's go to the cinema' said Jack.

2 (Jack/suggest) _____
_____.

It was 8.30 p.m. and the film had finished. 'Come on, Darren. Come for a pizza,' said Natalie.

3 (Natalie/persuade) _____
_____.

It was 9.45. Darren was outside his house. What should he do?

4 (should/he/deny/be/late) _____
_____?

5 (should/he/apologise/be/late) _____
_____?

Suddenly, Darren's parents arrived home in a taxi. 'Where have you been? I've been here for an hour! I've been worried,' said Darren.

6 (Darren/ask) _____
_____.

7 (he/tell) _____ and that _____
_____.

3 Report what the singer said. Use the verbs in the box.

• deny • refuse • ~~apologise~~ • promise
• complain • admit

1 I'm sorry I didn't turn up at the concert yesterday.
2 The newspaper reviews of my last album were very unfair.
3 It's not true. I'm not making an album with Eminem.
4 Yes, it's true. I've got some personal problems.
5 Next year, I'll play more concerts in Britain.
6 No, I won't join Take This again. No way!

At singer William Robbie's press conference yesterday he …

1 _apologised for not turning up at the concert the previous day_.
2 _____.
3 _____.
4 _____.
5 _____.
6 _____.

4 ▭▭▭ **Look at and match the six people (1–6) to the correct reporting verbs (a–f). Then report what each person said.**

a) Paula Sweet (deny) [1]

b) Terry James (admit) [ ]

c) Ben Fisher (suggest) [ ]

d) Nick Tyler (apologise) [ ]

e) Jake Norris (promise) [ ]

f) Sara Philips (complain) [ ]

> I don't love Jack.

1 *Paula Sweet denied loving Jack.*

> Katie, I'll never leave you.

2 _____

> Dave, I'm sorry that I broke your MP3 player.

3 _____

> My boyfriend never gives me flowers!

4 _____

> Yes, it's true, I lied.

5 _____

> Let's go to the skatepark.

6 _____

Grammar summary

Reported speech with verbs of reporting

Followed by infinitive

She **told** us **not to talk** during the exam.

They **asked** us **to leave**.

He **refused to eat** his dinner.

Followed by gerund (-*ing* form)

Sara **admitted losing** my book.

I **suggested going** to the cinema.

Chris **apologised for waking** us up.

Followed by *that* and a clause

Harry **explained that** he **had missed** the bus.

Seth **denied that** he **had broken** the phone.

Nick **suggested that** we **went** home.

Note

Form

- There are different reporting verb forms.
  - With verbs such as *ask*, *tell*, *invite*, *persuade*, *encourage*, *refuse*, *agree*, *promise* and *order* we use the structure:
    reporting verb + (*not*) + *to* + infinitive.
    He **invited** us **to go** to his party.
    They **agreed not to tell** anyone.
  - With verbs such as *admit*, *deny*, *suggest* and *apologise* we use the structure:
    reporting verb + (*not*) + gerund (-*ing* form).
    Some verbs are followed by a preposition,
    e.g. *apologise for*.
    He **suggested leaving** early.
    They **apologised for making** a lot of noise.
  - With verbs such as *deny*, *complain*, *explain*, *suggest* and *admit* we use the structure:
    reporting verb + *that* + clause.
    He **explained that** he had been busy.
  - Some reporting verbs have more than one possible structure with no change in meaning.
    She **denied being** responsible.
    She **denied that she was** responsible.

7c In spite of your faults, …

Vocabulary: Relationship words and phrases

1 ⭐ **Complete the crossword.**

Across

2 and 3: keep _____ _____ with someone

5 make _____ with someone after an argument

6 _____ someone out on a date

7 _____ divorced from someone

8 get engaged _____ someone

Down

7 and 1: _____ out *with* someone

3 _____ someone with your secrets

4 be _____ to someone

```
          ┌─┐
          │¹│
          │w│
        ┌─┼─┤
        │²│ │
        │i│ │
        ├─┤ │
  ┌─┬─┐ │t│
  │³│ │⁴│h│
  └─┴─┴─┤ │
  ┌─┐   │ │
  │⁵│   │ │
  ├─┴─┬─┤ │
  │   │⁶│ │
┌─┤   │ │ │
│⁷│   │ │
├─┤   └─┘
│⁸│
└─┘
```

2 ⭐⭐ **Complete the texts with relationship words and phrases.**

YOUR PROBLEMS ANSWERED

I get ¹*on* well with a boy in my class, but I don't want to go ²_____ with him. He doesn't understand.   Mel

Our advice

My older sister ⁸_____ engaged to Joe on her eighteenth birthday. She's going to get married ⁹_____ him this summer. He's ten years older than she is. I'm worried. I'm sure he's not right for her.   Phil

Our advice

I met a girl at a party and I ³_____ in love ⁴_____ her as soon as I saw her. I asked her ⁵_____ and she said 'Yes', but at the moment we're ⁶_____ lots of arguments and I'm worried that we're going to break ⁷_____ soon.   Aaron

Our advice

My best friend left our school and I've ¹⁰_____ touch with him. We were very ¹¹_____ friends and I really want to get in touch again, but he's not on Facebook or anything and I don't know his address. What can I do?   Dave

Our advice

Grammar: Clauses and linkers of contrast

3 ⭐ **Choose the correct options.**

1 **Although** / **Despite** / **However** I like my parents, they sometimes annoy me.

2 **Despite** / **In spite** / **Although** of being quite good looking, I can't get a girlfriend.

3 **However** / **Although** / **Despite** arguing all the time, my brother and I are very close.

4 One girl in my class is really pretty and really clever. **Although** / **However** / **Despite**, she isn't very friendly.

5 My parents can be quite strict during the school year. **On the other hand** / **Although** / **In spite of**, they give me a lot of freedom in the holidays.

6 **Despite** / **In spite of** / **Although** my boyfriend likes playing sport, he also spends a lot of time playing computer games.

4 ★★ Link the sentences using the word or phrase in brackets.

Successful film series. Part 4.

The Twilight Saga

The Twilight Saga is a series of five films.

1 The Twilight Saga didn't get very good reviews. It was incredibly popular. (although)
Although the Twilight Saga didn't get very good reviews, it was incredibly popular.

2 *Twilight* is considered to be a romance. Teenagers who don't like love stories also enjoyed it. (on the other hand)
_____

3 The film features vampires and werewolves. It is for all ages. (However)
_____

4 I was disappointed with the dialogues. I thought the special effects were great. (although)
_____

5 I didn't enjoy the first three films very much. I had to see how it all ended. (despite)
_____

6 The Twilight Saga was disappointing. Robert Pattinson and Kristen Stewart have become very rich because of it. (however)
_____

Grammar summary

Clauses and linkers of contrast

Although we were tired, we finished our work.
In spite of being tired, we finished our work.
Despite being tired, we finished our work.
We were tired. **However,** we finished our work.
We wanted to stop work. **On the other hand**, we wanted to finish before we went to bed.

Note

Use
- We use these words and phrases to contrast two ideas.
  Although I enjoyed the film, I don't want to see the second part.

Form
- *Although* can come at the beginning of a sentence or between the two ideas.
  Although I was late, I didn't get into trouble.
  I didn't get into trouble although I was late.
- *Despite* and *in spite of* are followed by the gerund (-*ing* form) of the verb.
  Despite having lots of arguments, they didn't split up.
- We usually start a second sentence which contrasts with the first with *however* or *on the other hand*.
  We went out a few times. However, we were never really in love.
  She might say yes. On the other hand, she might not.

Common mistakes
Despite I am an only child, I'm never lonely. ✗
Despite being an only child, I'm never lonely. ✓
Although I am an only child, I'm never lonely. ✓

7 Language round-up

1 Choose the correct options.

Matt
Debbie called. She said that she ¹**has** / **had** rung twice, but you ²**didn't get** / **hadn't got** back to her. She asked ³**are you** / **if you were** all right. I ⁴**said** / **told** her that you ⁵**had gone** / **have gone** out and had left your phone at home. I said that you ⁶**will** / **would** be back at about nine. She promised ⁷**ringing** / **to ring** back later.

Matt
Debbie rang again. She said that she ⁸**is** / **was** going to bed early so might not be awake when you get home. She ⁹**said** / **told** that she ¹⁰**hasn't got** / **didn't have** any important news, but just ¹¹**wanted** / **wants** to chat.

Matt
Debbie rang (again)! She wanted to know if you ¹²**can** / **could** send her the link to the website you ¹³**told** / **said** her about at school. Can you tell your friend that I'm your sister not your secretary?!

.../12

2 Complete the texts with one word in each gap.

YOUR PROBLEMS ANSWERED

PROBLEM
I have a friend at school who I've always ¹g*ot* on well with. I've always known that he will be ²t_____ for me if I need him and he knows that he can ³t_____ me with his secrets. The problem is that, recently, he has asked me ⁴o_____ on a date. ⁵A_____ we're very ⁶c_____ friends, I'm not in love with him. I tried to explain to him that I ⁷w_____ rather just stay friends than become boyfriend/girlfriend, but he ⁸k_____ asking me and I don't know what to do.

OUR ADVICE
It's a difficult problem. You may discover that you are right for each other. On the other ⁹h_____ it may destroy your friendship, especially if you start ¹⁰g_____ out and then ¹¹b_____ up or meet someone else. It's important to explain exactly how you feel and don't make him think that he has a chance of romance if it isn't going to happen. Good luck!

.../10

3 Complete the text with the words from the box. Put the verbs in the correct form.

- engaged • make • break • send • that
- have • talk • meet • dance • apologise
- not be • take • be

Dear Elaine,
Mark and I have just got ¹*engaged*! We'd had an argument on Saturday. He rang me in the afternoon and said that he ²_____ going out with his friends ³_____ evening. He'd promised ⁴_____ me out, so you can imagine how I felt. I told him I ⁵_____ going to stay at home on my own and I went to a disco with Sarah, where a boy asked me ⁶_____. While we were dancing, I noticed Mark dancing with another girl. That's when we ⁷_____ the argument and ⁸_____ up. The next day, he phoned to ⁹_____ for what had happened, but I refused ¹⁰_____ to him. He kept ¹¹_____ me text messages and, finally, I agreed ¹²_____ him at a restaurant, where he gave me the ring. What a way to ¹³_____ up with each other!
All the best
Annie

.../12

4 Make full sentences from the prompts.

1 Melanie/invite/we/spend/the weekend at her parents' beach house

Melanie invited us to spend the weekend at her parents' beach house.

2 Our teacher/promise/not give/we/homework on Fridays

_____

3 My mum/suggest/go/shopping together, but I/tell/she/I/not want to

_____

4 Despite/not do/much work/my brother manage/pass/his exams last June

_____

.../6

🎧 **LISTEN AND CHECK YOUR SCORE**	
Total	.../40

7 Skills practice

SKILLS FOCUS: READING AND **WRITING**

Read

1 **Read the texts and match the facts (1–4) to Lily (L) or Ashton (A).**

1 He/She has had a number one album. ☐ L

2 He/She is now divorced. ☐

3 He/She gave a lot of money to help people. ☐

4 He/She used the internet to help his/her career. ☐

Lily Allen is one of Britain's most popular singers. When she was eleven years old, her music teacher heard her singing in the playground and started giving her lessons in the lunch hour. Before 2005, she wasn't very well-known, despite having a contract with a record company. She decided to put her songs onto the website, MySpace. Thousands of people heard them. Her popularity through MySpace led to magazine interviews and her record label finally realised that she could be a star. Since then, she has had a number one hit single, *Smile*, and a number one album, *It's not me, it's you*. Over thirty million people have now downloaded songs from her website and she has also sold millions of CDs.

Ashton Kutcher is an American actor who is best known for his role in the TV series *That '70s Show*. In 2003, he started going out with Demi Moore. They got married in 2005, but were divorced in 2013. Ashton is also famous because of Twitter. Ashton and the television channel CNN were both trying to become the first Twitter user to get one million followers. Ashton offered to give $100,000 to help fight malaria if he got a million followers first and he did. It was a great way for Twitter to get publicity as, at the time, it wasn't quite as popular as it is today (in 2013, Justin Bieber had forty million followers!).

2 **Read the text again and decide whether the statements are true (T), false (F) or if it doesn't say (DS).**

1 Lily Allen signed a recording contract while she was still at school. _DS_

2 She put songs onto MySpace because she couldn't get a record contract. ___

3 The song *Smile* was a track on the album, *It's not me, it's you*. ___

4 Ashton Kutcher and Demi Moore got married about two years after they started going out together. ___

5 Ashton Kutcher now has more followers on Twitter than CNN. ___

6 Ashton Kutcher is not the only person to have more than a million followers on Twitter. ___

Write

3 **Make sentences and then write the sentences in the correct order.**

Why make phone calls from your computer?

an very internet it's easy Secondly, to phone use

webcam speaker see a if Lastly, got they've you can the other

a make another Firstly, phone from one to free it's call to computer

1 *Firstly, it's free to make a phone call from one computer to another.*

2 _____

_____

3 _____

_____

4 **Write a blog about your favourite way of communicating with your friends. Say why you like this form of communication. Use *firstly*, *secondly* and *lastly* to separate your reasons and give as much detail as you can.**

8a He shouldn't have left it there.

Phrases

1 ⭐ **Complete the phrases.**

1 **Matt:** Do you think anyone will buy my computer?

   Simon: What? T_hat_ o_____ thing? I don't think so!

2 **Kylie:** My parents say that I have to be home by 10 p.m.

   Beth: W_____ a d_____! Malcolm's parties are always so good.

3 **Natalie:** Where's Mrs Taylor? She should be here by now.

   Cheryl: H_____ o_____. I'll see if she's in the staffroom.

Grammar: _should have/ought to have_

2 ⭐ **Complete the blog with the correct form of the verbs in brackets.**

Saturday November 10th

What a terrible week at school! I wish I could go back and change it. What did I do wrong? Here's my confession!

- Sunday: I shouldn't [1]_have stayed_ (stay) up so late. I was so tired on Monday!
- Monday: I ought [2]_____ (do) more revision for my exam. I did really badly!
- Tuesday: I should [3]_____ (listen) to my teacher. I didn't know what to do!
- Tuesday: I shouldn't [4]_____ (believe) Melanie's gossip about Susie. Her stories are never true!
- Wednesday: I ought not [5]_____ (switch on) my mobile phone in the English lesson. The teacher was really angry when it rang!
- Thursday: I should [6]_____ (go) straight home after school. Mum was worried and now she's going to collect me in the car every day.
- Friday: I ought [7]_____ (remember) my books. Now I have to write my notes from all my lessons into my notebooks.
- Friday: I shouldn't [8]_____ (write) notes to Maria during the French test. The teacher saw me and thought I was cheating.

3 ⭐⭐⭐ **Complete the email with the affirmative or negative form of _should_ (s) or _ought to_ (o) and the correct form of the verbs from the box.**

- look • take • wear • leave • ask
- make • allow • ~~plan~~ • buy • go

Hi Rhani,

Thanks for the email! Don't worry! It wasn't your fault that the weekend was a disaster.

We [1](s) _should have planned_ everything a bit more carefully. We definitely [2](o) _____ the bus tickets in advance. I didn't know the buses were so busy at the weekend. The driver [3](o) _____ us to stand. He [4](s) _____ us wait for two hours until the next bus arrived.

We [5](s) _____ at some websites before we left. It wasn't much fun trying to find somewhere to stay in the rain!

The walk on Sunday was nice, but, yes, you were right (again!)! We [6](o) _____ a map with us and we [7](s) _____ more comfortable shoes too – my feet were so sore! We [8](o) _____ to the gym more often last month, too. We are so unfit!

I'm sorry about the money, too. I [9](s) _____ it lying on the bed for everyone to see. I'm sure someone saw it there and stole it. It wasn't all bad though, was it? We met Mike and Tom. They were really nice and very funny! We [10](s) _____ them for their email addresses! Still, maybe we can look them up on Facebook!

Anyway, I must go now and do some school work!

See you soon!

Love,

Lizzie

Use your English: Apologise for past mistakes

4 ⭐ **Complete the dialogues with the words and phrases from the box.**

- so late • That's OK • so sorry • mind
- the state of • you been • At least
- back very late • all right • ~~waiting ages~~

Dialogue 1

Nathan: We've been ¹*waiting ages* for you. Why are you ²_____?

Elizabeth: I'm ³_____. I had to wait for my mum to come home.

Nathan: That's ⁴_____. The film hasn't started yet.

Dialogue 2

Mrs Hird: You're ⁵_____ from school. Where have ⁶_____?

Kelly: I'm sorry. We had extra practice for the school play and I didn't have my mobile phone with me.

Mrs Hird: ⁷_____. ⁸_____ you're back home safely.

Dialogue 3

Mr Grayson: Look at ⁹_____ your homework! What happened to it?

Peter: I'm really sorry. My little brother spilt his juice all over it.

Mr Grayson: Well, never ¹⁰_____. Do it again this evening and give it to me tomorrow.

Grammar summary

should have/ought to have

Affirmative
He **should have tried** harder.
You **ought to have known** what would happen.

Negative
I **shouldn't have been** so rude.
They **oughtn't to have shouted**.

Note

Use

- We use *should have* or *ought to have* to
  - talk about regrets about our own past actions.
    *I **shouldn't have worn** that dress to the party.*
  - criticise or give advice about other people's past actions.
    *You **should have finished** that an hour ago.*
    *You **ought to have seen** the film when it was on at the cinema.*

Form

- We use *should/ought to* + *have* + past participle.
  *We **should have left** earlier.*
- *Oughtn't* is often replaced by *ought not* in negative sentences.
  *You **ought not** to have bought that watch.* ✓
  *You **oughtn't** to have bought that watch.* ✓

Common mistakes

~~You shouldn't have went to bed so late.~~ ✗
You shouldn't have **gone** to bed so late. ✓
~~He ought have worked harder.~~ ✗
He ought **to** have worked harder. ✓

8b It can't be easy.

Vocabulary: Phrasal verbs with *away*

1 ⭐ **Choose the correct options.**

1 The thief ___ away and the police couldn't stop him.

   a) threw   b) ran   c) gave

2 Mr Smith ___ the tickets away accidentally.

   a) gave   b) put   c) threw

3 Jessica didn't like the scary bits so she ___ away from the TV.

   a) passed   b) looked   c) put

4 Toby ___ his old toys away to the charity shop.

   a) gave   b) put   c) threw

5 The students of class 5C are ___ their books away.

   a) throwing   b) passing   c) putting

6 The fish ___ away.

   a) got   b) threw   c) gave

Grammar: *must/can't/might/could* for deductions in the present

2 ⭐ **Match the sentences (1–12) to the correct reasons (a–l).**

1 He must be the new teacher.   a) I think we're getting one today.

2 He can't be the new teacher.   b) I saw him in the teachers' room.

3 He might be the new teacher.   c) He's too young.

4 There can't be a monster in here.   d) Anything's possible!

5 There might be a monster in here.   e) So many people have seen it.

6 There must be a monster in here.   f) Monsters don't exist.

7 Aliens can't really exist.   g) There are so many planets.

8 Aliens must exist.   h) I mean, why not?

9 Aliens might exist.   i) It's just impossible.

10 Rob might have got his new computer.   j) He looks very happy.

11 Rob can't have got his new computer.   k) Let's go and see.

12 Rob must have got his new computer.   l) He hasn't got enough money.

3 ⭐⭐⭐ Complete the dialogue with the correct modal and a verb from the box.

- find • be • have • love • ~~be~~ • think
- know • be

Rose: Hi Dan! What on earth are you doing looking in the rubbish bin? The concert starts in an hour.

Dan: I'm ... er looking for something.

Rose: What are you looking for? It ¹*must be* important for you to be doing it now. I thought you would be ready to go.

Dan: Well, I'm not ready because, you see, ehm, I've lost the tickets.

Rose: What! I don't believe you! Well, they ² _____ in the bin. You're always so careful. Why don't you look in your wallet? You ³ _____ them in there.

Dan: I thought of that. I've checked there twice.

Rose: I'll ask your mum. She ⁴ _____ where they are. She usually knows where things are.

Dan: She doesn't. I asked her earlier. I'm so sorry, Rose. You ⁵ _____ I'm really stupid!

Rose: Don't worry. I know. I'll look in your school jacket ... Dan, here they are!

Dan: Hang on! These are for tomorrow's concert.

Rose: Tomorrow? Are you going again, tomorrow? Wow! You ⁶ _____ *Bloc Party*.

Dan: I do. They're great. I'm going with my brother tomorrow. Hey! That's it! He ⁷ _____ today's tickets.

Rose: Great! Where is he? He ⁸ _____ here somewhere. I saw his bike outside and he never goes anywhere without that!

Dan: He's upstairs, in his room. Wait here and I'll get the tickets ...

Grammar summary

must/can't/might/could for deductions in the present
Certainty
I **must be dreaming**.
It **must be** his day off work.
She **can't go** to this school. It's a boys' school!
Possibility
The burglar **might be** upstairs.
You **might not win** the competition.
We **could** be the youngest people here.

Note

Use

- We use *must* when we are very sure something is true, although we don't know for a fact.
  *He **must be** the new student.* (I am sure, but I don't know for a fact.)

- We use *can't* when we are sure that something is not possible, although we don't know for a fact.
  *The Loch Ness Monster **can't** really exist.* (I'm sure of this, but I don't know for a fact.)

- We use *might* or *could* when something is possible, but we are not very sure.
  *They **might/could be** stuck in traffic.* (It is a possibility, but I'm not sure this is the reason they are late.)

Form

- We use *must/can't/might/could* + infinitive without *to*.
  *He **can't be** seventeen!*

Common mistakes

~~They can be teachers.~~ ✗
*They **might/could** be teachers.* ✓
~~He can't has his own computer.~~ ✗
*He can't **have** his own computer.* ✓

8c He can't have drowned.

Vocabulary: Crime

1 ⭐ **Match the beginnings (1–10) to the endings (a–j).**

1 Dan robbed   _g_

2 Sid burgled   ___

3 Jake broke   ___

4 Angela has never committed   ___

5 Fred vandalised   ___

6 Mrs Jenkins had to pay   ___

7 Sergeant Henderson arrested   ___

8 Annie stole   ___

9 Rick drew   ___

10 Mick mugged   ___

a) a crime.

b) graffiti all over the bus stop.

c) a fine.

d) three houses before he was caught.

e) the criminal and took him to the police station.

f) a bus stop.

g) the local bank.

h) €1,000 from a shop.

i) an old lady in the street.

j) into the post office at night.

2 ⭐ **Choose the correct options.**

1 The shop assistant accused Diane ___ stealing a bar of chocolate.

   (a) of   b) for   c) with

2 The police arrested my mum ___ driving too fast.

   a) with   b) of   c) for

3 Paul went ___ prison for three months.

   a) for   b) to   c) in

4 The police suspected my dad ___ being a burglar when he climbed through the window!

   a) of   b) with   c) for

5 The police charged Toby ___ vandalising the phone box.

   a) for   b) with   c) of

6 In court, Henry was convicted ___ stealing cars.

   a) with   b) of   c) for

Grammar: *must have/can't have/might have/could have* for deductions in the past

3 ⭐ **Complete the sentences with the verbs in brackets and *must have, can't have* or *might/could have.***

1 The burglar _must have climbed_ (climb) through the window.

2 We _____ (close) the window before we went out.

3 He _____ (try) to open the front door first, but that was locked.

4 The burglar _____ (go) into any of the bedrooms because there are no footprints upstairs.

5 He _____ (have) dirty boots on.

6 He _____ (walk) across the garden. Let's go and see if there are any footprints there.

7 The burglar _____ (hear) a noise and left in a hurry.

8 He _____ (see) the computer. It's still here on the desk.

9 He walked straight to the painting. He _____ (know) that the money was behind it.

4 ▦▦▦ **Read the texts and make deductions using the prompts and *must have, can't have* or *might/could have*.**

The Gardner Museum Mystery

What we know

Thirteen paintings disappeared worth $200 million. The police have never caught the thieves. They are sure that the paintings are now in Europe. They think the criminals sold them secretly. There is no way the criminals have still got them because they want the money not the paintings. One theory is that a local group of criminals organised the crime, but no one really knows. Whoever it was knew exactly what they were doing. Only very clever criminals could have done what they did.

1 The criminals/sell the paintings

   The criminals must have sold the paintings.

2 The criminals/keep the paintings

   _____

3 A local group of criminals/organise the crime

   _____

4 The criminals/be very clever

   _____

The mystery of Stonehenge

What we know

Approximately 4,000 years ago, someone transported these giant stones hundreds of kilometres. It almost certainly took many years to complete. No one really knows what it was for. One theory is that it was for watching the stars. The only thing we can be sure of is that it was definitely important.

5 Stonehenge/be important

   _____

6 It/be easy to build

   _____

7 People/use it for watching the stars

   _____

8 It/take a long time to complete

   _____

Grammar summary

must have/can't have/might have/could have for deductions in the past
Certainty
They **must have gone** the wrong way.
You **can't have locked** the door.
Possibility
I **could have phoned** the wrong number.
She **might not have heard** the phone.

Note

Use

- We use *must have* when we are very sure something about the past is true, although we don't know for a fact.

  *He **must have enjoyed** the film.* (I am sure, but I don't know for a fact.)

- We use *can't have* when we are sure that something didn't happen in the past, although we don't know for a fact.

  *Max **can't have robbed** the bank.* (I'm sure of this, but I don't know for a fact.)

- We use *might/could have* when something about the past is possible, but we are not very sure that it happened.

  *They **might/could have forgotten** their phone.* (It is a possibility, but I'm not sure this is the reason they haven't phoned us.)

Form

- We use *must have, can't have, might/could have* + past participle.

  *She **can't have written** this letter.*
  *He **might/could have gone** home.*
  *You **must have upset** him.*

Common mistakes

~~They must have went home.~~ ✗
They must have **gone** home. ✓
~~The burglar can have climbed through the window.~~ ✗
The burglar **might/could** have climbed through the window. ✓

8 Language round-up

1 Complete the dialogues with one word in each gap.

A: I can't come to your party tonight. I should ¹*have* told you earlier. Sorry.

B: ²_____'s OK. Sorry you can't come.

C: I ought ³_____ to have been rude about your new haircut. Sorry.

D: That's ⁴_____ right. ⁵_____ least you told the truth!

E: I ought ⁶_____ have worked harder for these exams. They're really difficult.

F: Never ⁷_____. You must ⁸_____ glad that the summer holidays will start soon.

G: I'm really ⁹_____ about last night. It can't have ¹⁰_____ easy listening to my problems.

H: I hope I helped. You ¹¹_____ to have told me about them earlier.

.../10

2 Complete the text with the correct form of the words in capitals.

There are more and more crimes in our area. The library was ¹*vandalised* (VANDAL) and some books were ²_____ (STEAL). The problem is that ³_____ (CRIME) aren't afraid of the police. My aunt was attacked by a ⁴_____ (MUG) and a ⁵_____ (BURGLE) got into our house one night and took the television. He must have ⁶_____ (CLIMB) in through the bathroom window. I know we should have ⁷_____ (CLOSE) it, but we didn't think anyone could get in there. He must have ⁸_____ (BE) very small! We should have ⁹_____ (LEAVE) the area a few years ago when it started to become more dangerous. We could still sell the house. There must ¹⁰_____ (BE) someone who wants to live here and doesn't know how much crime there is. Or maybe a ¹¹_____ (THEFT) would like to live here to be close to his work!

.../10

3 Complete the sentences with the correct form of the verbs from the box.

• ~~put~~ • draw • commit • accuse • steal
• arrest • run • get • charge • go • throw

1 *Put* your books away and leave quietly.
2 Mum has _____ my old jeans away.
3 The police _____ Mr Smith last week for _____ graffiti on the school wall.
4 Would you cheat in an exam if you thought you could _____ away with it?
5 Someone has _____ my mobile phone!
6 The boys were _____ with vandalism.
7 Mark _____ away from the fire.
8 Have you ever _____ a crime?
9 I was _____ of lying, but it wasn't true.
10 They've _____ away for a few days.

.../10

4 Complete the second sentence to mean the same as the first. Use the word in capitals.

1 It was a mistake for me to eat so much cake. SHOULDN'T
   I *shouldn't have eaten* so much cake.

2 It would have been better if you had worn a coat. OUGHT
   You _____ a coat.

3 I'm certain that this is the right address. BE
   This _____ address.

4 I'm sure we aren't late. BE
   We _____.

5 Perhaps it was a student at the school. COULD
   It _____ _____ at the school.

6 The thief escaped from the police. GOT
   The thief _____ the police.

.../10

🔊 LISTEN AND CHECK YOUR SCORE

Total	.../40

8 Skills practice

SKILLS FOCUS: READING, LISTENING AND **WRITING**

Read

1 **Read the texts and complete the facts.**

1 Cheryl Cole:

Activity: [1]*Climbed Mount Kilimanjaro*

Raised money for: [2]_____

2 Jennifer Lopez:

Activity: [3]_____

Raised money for: [4]_____

Cheryl Cole, the singer, was one of nine celebrities who reached the top of Mount Kilimanjaro yesterday. They climbed the mountain to raise money to buy mosquito nets for Tanzania. These will help stop malaria. So far, they have raised over a million pounds. The climb took five days altogether. The celebrities left the last camp just after midnight so that they were able to reach the top in time to see the sun rise.

Jennifer Lopez has helped to raise $127,000. The money will be given to a children's hospital in Los Angeles. Jennifer took part in a sponsored triathlon. The three events were a one-kilometre swim, a twenty-five-kilometre bike ride and a six-kilometre run. Jennifer's time was two hours and twenty-three minutes. Speaking to reporters, Jennifer said that she was delighted to have finished, but hadn't realised how difficult the swimming part would be.

2 **Read the texts again and write what the numbers refer to.**

1 9: *Nine celebrities climbed Mount Kilimanjaro.*

2 1,000,000+: _____

3 5: _____

4 127,000: _____

5 1, 25, 6: _____

6 2h 23m: _____

Listen

3 (13) **Match the speakers (1–4) with the ideas for raising money (a–d).**

Speaker 1	a) selling tickets to a party
Speaker 2	b) selling things at an auction
Speaker 3	c) holding a sponsored dance
Speaker 4	d) face-painting

4 (13) **Listen again and complete the sentences.**

1 The first speaker thinks their idea is more fun than a *walk* or *swim*.

2 The last time they held the event it lasted from _____ until _____.

3 The second speaker's idea needs volunteers to do things like decorating, being the _____ and _____ after the party.

4 The third speaker thinks they can charge £ _____ for each person they paint.

5 The fourth speaker _____ some great things at the auction.

Write

5 **Look at the advert. Write a formal letter of application for a place as a volunteer on the sports camp.**

★ US Summer Sports Camp ★

Volunteers needed

We need young people aged fifteen to twenty-one to help on our summer sports camps.
You need to be: * fit and healthy * imaginative
* friendly * hard-working * enthusiastic
* good with children (aged six to twelve)

Responsibilities

* Organising sports events for the children.
* Organising afternoon and evening social events.
* Helping all students enjoy their time at camp.

9a The telephone was invented.

Grammar: The passive: present simple, past simple, present perfect, past perfect

1 ⭐ **Choose the active or passive form.**

Some stars ¹(**like**) / **are liked** the paparazzi because they make them feel important. Their photographs ²**publish / are published** in many magazines and newspapers all over the world. Photographers ³**often pay / are often paid** thousands of pounds by these magazines and newspapers. However, celebrities sometimes get so angry with the paparazzi that they ⁴**attack / are attacked** them. Recently, one photographer ⁵**claimed / was claimed** that Keanu Reeves had attacked him. He said that he ⁶**had hurt / had been hurt** and couldn't work. Keanu Reeves ⁷**didn't believe / wasn't believed** him and wanted to show that the photographer was lying. So, the photographer ⁸**filmed / was filmed** secretly by a private detective. The photographer was working and he was still taking photographs. There was nothing wrong with him! In the end, Keanu was right after all.

2 ⭐⭐ **Change the active sentences into the passive. Use *by* + agent where necessary.**

1 My friend wrote this article.
   This article was written by my friend.

2 Millions of viewers watched the new reality TV programme.

   _____

3 Photographers photographed Brad Pitt as he left the restaurant.

   _____

4 My friends didn't tell me about the party.

   _____

5 Our teacher has given us lots of homework this week.

   _____

6 Jack Stevens from Class 5 wrote the graffiti on the school wall.

   _____

3 ⭐⭐ **Complete the text with the correct passive form of the verbs in brackets.**

Where does the word 'paparazzi' come from? What does it mean? It ¹*was* first *used* (use) in 1960 in an Italian film. The film ² _____ (call) *La Dolce Vita*. One of the characters in the film was a photographer and the character ³ _____ (give) the name Paparazzo by the director Federico Fellini. In Italian, this means an annoying noise. It is the sound that ⁴ _____ (make) by a mosquito. Fellini ⁵ _____ (ask) in an interview why he chose that name and he said that he had gone to school with a boy who ⁶ _____ (give) the nickname Paparazzo by his friends. However, Fellini may have got the idea from somewhere else. Ennio Flaiano, who worked with Fellini, said that they had found the name in a book which ⁷ _____ (write) long before Fellini's film. It's not really important where the idea came from. Since *La Dolce Vita* ⁸ _____ first _____ (show) in 1960, the word paparazzo ⁹ _____ (use) all over the world to describe news photographers.

4 ▓▓▓▓ **Make questions and sentences from the prompts.**

1 Who/this headline/write/by?

   Who was this headline written by?

2 Three journalists/just arrest/the police.

   _____

3 Before it appeared in the newspapers, this article/publish/online all over the world.

   _____

4 This magazine/publish/online every week, but I prefer to buy the paper copy.

   _____

5 Every story in the online paper/follow/ comments from readers.

   _____

6 How many blogs/write/every day?

   _____

Vocabulary: The media

5 ▓▓▓ **Complete the words with one letter in each gap.**

1 Let's look at the *h e a d l i n e s* from this morning's papers.

2 And here's Jon Bishop with a l __ __ e r __ __ __ __ t from the White House.

3 Do we need new laws to protect us from the p __ __ __ __ s?

4 We're just getting an u __ __ __ __ e from London.

5 You don't get your fingers dirty when you read an o __ __ __ __ e newspaper!

6 Here's a news b __ __ __ __ __ __ n from the earthquake-affected city.

7 Which forms of s __ __ __ __ l m __ __ __ a will we be using next year?

Grammar summary

The passive: present simple, past simple, present perfect, past perfect
Affirmative & Negative
I **am (not) driven** to school (by my parents).
We **are (not) given** lots of homework (by our teacher).
He **was (not) introduced** to all the guests.
They **were (not) shown** a film.
You **have (not) been told** to clean up the mess.
She **has (not) been sentenced** to prison.
He **had (not) been recognised**.
Questions
Is this programme **shown** on satellite TV?
Was he **followed** by journalists?
Have we **been given** the wrong information?
Had you **been informed**?

Note

Use

- We use the passive to say what is, was or has been done to a person.
- We use the passive when
  - we don't know the subject.
    *Our house **was burgled**.*
  - the action or the object is more important than the subject.
    *We had left the school when we **were told** to be quiet.*
  - we want to avoid mentioning who did something.
    *Mistakes **have been made**, but now everything is all right.*

Form

- We form the present and past passive with the correct form of *to be* + the past participle of the verb.
  *We **are given** homework every day.*
  *The criminal **was sentenced** to ten years in prison.*
- If it is important to say who or what the agent (= subject) is/was, we use *by*.
  *We are given homework every day **by our teacher**.*
  *The burglar was sentenced **by the judge**.*
- We form the present and past perfect passive by using *have/has been* or *had been* + past participle.
  *We**'ve been given** the wrong map!*
  *It was the first time I **had been asked** for my autograph.*

9b They're being followed.

Phrases

1a ⭐☆☆ Choose the correct option.

1 What **more** / **much** / **many** do you want?

2 What's going **up** / **out** / **on**?

3 Dream **off** / **on** / **out**!

4 I don't like rock music that **many** / **much** / **a lot**.

1b ⭐⭐☆ Complete the dialogue with the correct phrases from Exercise 1a.

George: Hey, Harry! What are you up to just now?

Harry: Nothing much. Why?

George: Come to the CD shop with me.

Harry: Why? ¹*What's going on?*

George: Robbie Strange is there. He's giving away free copies of his CD.

Harry: Robbie Strange? No way! Robbie Strange, here in Horsham, the most boring town in England!

George: Yeah, I know. I couldn't believe it. So, do you want to come?

Harry: I'm not sure. Anyway, I don't like Robbie Strange ²_____.

George: Harry, there's a big pop star in our town and you're not sure? ³_____

Harry: The Sugababes! I want the Sugababes to come to Horsham! I could talk to them, invite them to my party even.

George: ⁴_____ I don't think the Sugababes are going to go to your party!

Grammar: The passive: present continuous, past continuous and future simple

2 ⭐☆☆ Complete the newspaper articles with the phrases from the box.

> • were being followed • is being examined
> • were being filmed • will be allowed
> • are being looked at • was being driven

Star News

Toby Francis, the *Big Brother* winner, ¹*is being examined* in a Manchester hospital today after a car accident. He is not believed to be badly hurt. He ²_____ to the TV studios for a chat show when another car crashed into his. The driver of the other car has been arrested for driving while using a mobile phone. According to hospital reports, Toby and his driver ³_____ to leave the hospital later today.

Star's holiday hell! Model Becky Lester was with her boyfriend when they realised that they ⁴_____ by a gang of muggers. Luckily, they ⁵_____ secretly at the time by paparazzi. The photographs ⁶_____ by the police, who are trying to see the faces of the muggers.

3 ⭐⭐☆ Complete the dialogues with the correct passive form of the verbs in brackets.

Dialogue 1

Student: Miss Smith. Have you decided who will play Romeo in the school play yet?

Teacher: Yes, I have. Romeo ¹*will be played* (play) by Martin Finch.

Student: Are the costumes ready?

Teacher: Not yet. They ²_____ (finish) at the moment.

Student: Why are they taking such a long time? They ³_____ (make) when we had our first meeting three weeks ago.

Teacher: Miss Davies is very busy, but they ⁴_____ (finish) very soon.

Dialogue 2

Editor: Where's the new model?

Secretary: She ⁵_____ (photograph) by the
            fashion photographer at the moment.

Editor: Why didn't he wait for me to arrive?

Secretary: You ⁶_____ (interview) so I told
            him to start.

Editor: OK. Let me see the photos as soon as they're ready.

Secretary: Of course. You ⁷_____ (show)
            the photos before lunch, I promise.

Use your English: Give opinions, agree and disagree

4 🌟 **Complete the dialogue with the words from the box.**

> • opinion • it's • sure • point • disagree • way • idea
> • too • agree

Tom: Hello Henry. Do you fancy coming to the debating
         society with me now?

Henry: I don't know. What do you do there? Can you give me
         an example?

Tom: OK. In my ¹*opinion*, we should learn more about
         politics in school.

Henry: I'm not ²_____ I ³_____ with you. The
         timetable is full. We can't have fewer Maths or English
         lessons because we need to study for our exams.

Tom: I take your ⁴_____. Maybe it shouldn't be a
         school subject, but I still think politics would be an
         interesting thing to talk about at school. We could have
         an after-school politics club.

Henry: Sorry, I ⁵_____. I think ⁶_____ a terrible
         ⁷_____. We're children! I think we should play
         more sports or just go home and watch TV.

Tom: Me ⁸_____.

Henry: What? But you said …

Tom: I was showing you what the debating society is like.
         You should come. You're good at it.

Henry: No ⁹_____! The only thing I want to debate is
         what computer game to play with my brother.

Grammar summary

The passive: present continuous, past continuous and future simple

Affirmative

I **am being followed**.
They **are being arrested**.
He **was being taken** to the hospital.
We **were being interviewed** by a
journalist.
You **will be given** a part in the new
film.

Negative

We **are not being interviewed** today.
She **isn't being chased** by a robber.
He **wasn't being shown** around the
factory.
They **weren't being interviewed**.
I **won't be seen** in the new film.

Questions

Are they **being questioned** by police?
Is it **being filmed** in London?
Was she **being told** what to do?
Were you **being asked** lots of
questions?
Will we **be shown** the photographs?

Note

Use

• See Unit 9a page 69.

Form

• We form the present and past
  continuous passive by using *am/is/are*
  or *was/were* + *being* + past participle.
  *My baby brother **is being fed** at the
  moment.*
  *The police **were being attacked** by
  angry workers.*

• We form the future simple passive by
  using *will* + *be* + past participle.
  *The students **will be given** their exam
  results tomorrow.*

Common mistakes

~~They were being telling what to do.~~ ✗
*They were being **told** what to do.* ✓

9c It ought to be stopped.

Grammar: The passive: modals, gerund (-ing form) and infinitive

1 ⭐ **Choose the correct options.**

School rules

1 Uniforms must **be worn** / **worn** / **being worn** at all times.
2 Homework has to **be done** / **being done** / **do** every day.
3 Students who arrive late should **to be sent** / **being sent** / **be sent** to the head teacher by their teachers.
4 All messages from the school to parents must **to be signed** / **be signed** / **be signing** by parents and returned to teachers.
5 Students shouldn't go into the staffroom without **being asked** / **be asked** / **to be asked**.
6 Tests ought to **mark** / **be marked** / **be mark** and returned to students in one week or less.
7 Ball games mustn't **play** / **be played** / **be playing** inside the school building.
8 Tests should **give** / **be giving** / **be given** once a term.
9 Teachers and students don't enjoy **being shouted** / **to be shouted** / **shouting** at. Please try to talk calmly and politely at all times.

2 ⭐⭐ **Complete the web comments with the correct passive form of the verbs in brackets.**

http://www.interestingopinions.com

www.interestingopinions.com

The website where you can write your opinions on any topic you like. Click on any statement that you'd like to agree or disagree with and tell us what you think and why.

Education

Some of our teachers look terrible. I think teachers should [1]_be given_ (give) uniforms to wear. *Melanie, age 14*

We should [2]_____ (tell) about tests in advance. Students don't like [3]_____ (give) surprise tests. *Dave, age 13*

Why aren't there more parents' evenings? Parents want [4]_____ (tell) about problems quickly. *Cathy, age 14*

The media

In the morning, I never have time to go to the newsagents. Newspapers ought [5]_____ (sell) at bus stops. *Keith, age 16*

Why do people read tabloid newspapers? They must enjoy [6]_____ (lie) to! *Tim, age 15*

Now that my family have moved to Italy, I can't watch the football on the BBC website. Sports shows shouldn't just [7]_____ (broadcast) in Britain! *Brett, age 14*

Work

It's difficult to bring up children and to work. Parents of young children should [8]_____ (allow) to work from home. *Cherie, age 17*

Who says that a footballer is worth more than a nurse? Or a doctor is worth more than a teacher? Everyone should [9]_____ (pay) the same wages. *Jack, age 14*

I hate wearing a uniform to school and I'm going to hate [10]_____ (make) to wear a tie at work. People should wear what they like to work. *Chris, age 15*

Vocabulary: Adjective and noun formation

3a ⭐ **Write (N) nouns or (A) adjectives.**

1 beautiful	_A_		6 wisdom	__
2 greed	__		7 cruelty	__
3 height	__		8 brave	__
4 courageous	__		9 poverty	__
5 angry	__		10 young	__

3b ⭐ **Complete the nouns and adjectives that match the words in Exercise 3a.**

1 b _e a u t y_   6 w __ __ __

2 g __ __ __ __ __   7 c __ __ __ __

3 h __ __ __   8 b __ __ __ __ __ __

4 c __ __ __ __ __   9 p __ __ __

5 a __ __ __ __   10 y __ __ __ __

4 ⭐⭐⭐ **Complete the text with the correct form of the words in brackets.**

What a show!

This year's final of *Our School's Got Talent* was very ¹_successful_ (success). Ten ²_____ (luck) students waited to show us what they could do while their ³_____ (pride) parents sat and watched them nervously. It was a ⁴_____ (stress) time for the students who were all ⁵_____ (hope) that they would win first prize.

Of course, there could only be one winner and that was Kathy Jenkins, aged fourteen. Her obvious ⁶_____ (confident) helped her, but the fact that she is also a brilliant singer and the most talented of the ten meant she was the judges' choice.

Eleven-year-old Luke Wright should also be given a special mention. Luke showed great ⁷_____ (courageous) entering the competition with students much older than himself. I'm sure he'll be back next year!

Grammar summary

The passive: modals, gerund (*-ing* form) and infinitive
Modals
I **should be given** the prize.
He **must be stopped**!
We **ought to be told**.
Gerund (*-ing*) form
She hates **being laughed** at.
They don't mind **being asked** lots of questions.
Being photographed by the paparazzi is a problem for some celebrities.
Infinitive
We want **to be given** more time.
Don't wait **to be asked**.

Note

Use

- See Unit 9a page 69.

Form

- We form modal passives by using a modal verb + *be* + past participle.
  *This project **must be done** tonight.*
- We form the passive of verbs which are followed by the *-ing* form in active sentences by using verb + *being* + past participle.
  *I **love being invited** to parties.*
- We form the passive of verbs which are followed by the infinitive in active sentences by using verb + *to be* + past participle.
  *You **have to be told** twice before you do anything.*

Common mistakes

~~I want to given a prize.~~ ✗
I want **to be given** a prize. ✓
~~I don't mind be asked for my autograph.~~ ✗
I don't mind **being asked** for my autograph. ✓

1 Choose the correct options.

When a new book ¹**is making** / **is being written** or a film ²**is making** / **is being made**, there has to be great secrecy.

Before JK Rowling ³**wrote** / **was written** the last Harry Potter book, hundreds of pages 'from the book' ⁴**published** / **were published** online. Some people claimed that her bins ⁵**had searched** / **had been searched** by people trying to find her notes. Some people say the book should have stayed a secret until it reached the shops. I'm not ⁶**agree** / **sure**. I take their ⁷**idea** / **point**, but if people want to spoil it for themselves, why shouldn't they? Film makers employ security guards to make sure that only people who ⁸**employ** / **are employed** in the studios can get in. However, even employees may ⁹**pay** / **be paid** for information by the newspapers. One thing is for sure. When the next blockbuster film is released, it ¹⁰**will watch** / **will be watched** all over the world weeks before it reaches the cinema.

.../9

2 Complete the story with the correct form of the verbs in brackets.

The two film stars, Jack and Pamela ¹_had been arrested_ (arrest) two hours earlier when they ²_____ (stop) by police for driving at 150 kph. When they ³_____ (ask) why they had been driving so fast they explained. 'We ⁴_____ (chase) by photographers,' answered Jack. 'We didn't want ⁵_____ (photograph) together. We ⁶_____ (already / tell) three times by the head of the film studio that our relationship should ⁷_____ (keep) secret.' 'Don't worry,' said the policeman, 'a car is coming for you. You ⁸_____ (collect) in about thirty minutes.' Jack and Pamela ⁹_____ (take) to a small room where they waited for the car.

The happy ending
Jack and Pamela
¹⁰_____
(drive) to the studio in a big, black car and their relationship stayed a secret.

The unhappy ending
Before Jack and Pamela left, a photographer
¹¹_____
(put) into the same room as them ...

.../10

3 Complete the text with the correct form of the words from the box.

• true • different • ~~be~~ • success • greed
• proud • anger • be

I don't like ¹_being_ made to wear a uniform to school, but we have to. The school says we should have ²_____ in our school and the uniform. So why don't the teachers wear a uniform?   *Natalie, age 14*

I don't believe newspapers tell lies. Celebrities would get ³_____ and do something about it. Just because you're famous and ⁴_____ doesn't mean people can lie about you. I think newspapers tell the ⁵_____.   *Keith, age 13*

I hate it when people say doctors earn too much. There's a big ⁶_____ between the work that a doctor does and what most people do. Doctors aren't ⁷_____, but their studies are expensive and that money has ⁸_____ paid back to the bank.   *Susie, age 14*

.../7

4 Make questions and answers from the prompts.

1 Have the Olympics ever/hold/in Australia?
   Have the Olympics ever been held in Australia?
   ✓ They/hold/in Sydney and in Melbourne.
   _____

2 Who/*Romeo and Juliet*/write/by?
   _____
   It/write/William Shakespeare.
   _____

3 *Mamma Mia*/sing/The Beatles?
   _____
   ✗ It/sing/Abba.
   _____

4 fish/eat/at Thanksgiving in America?
   _____
   ✗ Turkey/eat/at Thanksgiving in America.
   _____

.../14

🎧 **LISTEN AND CHECK YOUR SCORE**	
Total	.../40

9 Skills practice

SKILLS FOCUS: READING AND **WRITING**

Read

1 Match the headings (1–3) to the texts (A–C).

1 I need people to help me. ☐

2 Learn about working in a large shop. ☐

3 Have fun and learn interesting facts. ☐

A

Do you like working outside? Why not help out in your local zoo this summer? We need volunteers to feed the animals, clean the cages and keep the zoo looking tidy. It's great fun and you'll learn a lot about how animals live and how we look after them. No pay, but meals are provided.

B

Researchers required by busy politician. I'm looking for three young people to research articles on the internet, correct facts and spelling mistakes in my blog and update my website. There may be other duties such as answering the phone. Some travel may be necessary. I will pay for all transport, hotels and food.

C

Summer workers needed. On our management training scheme you will work in all departments of the store. Duties will include customer service, ordering and shelf filling. Show the right qualities and you may be offered university sponsorship and a job in one of our shops after completing your studies.

2 Read the texts again and match the questions to the correct job adverts.

Which job …

1 doesn't mention food? _C_

2 might offer work in the future? ___

3 could involve travel? ___

4 helps people to learn about animals? ___

5 needs someone to use a computer? ___

6 means you will work outside all the time? ___

Write

3 Complete the letter with the words from the box.

• interested • ~~summer~~ • sure • example
• that • shop

Dear Sam,

I heard from your mother that you are looking for some kind of ¹_summer_ work. I know a few people in business and I'm ²_____ that I could 'have a word in their ears'. Let me know what kind of work you want (office, ³_____, outdoors, restaurant, summer school) and what you want from it, for ⁴_____, money, something to put on your CV, exciting experiences, etc.

Also, I know I haven't seen you for a long time so tell me about yourself. What are you ⁵_____ in? Do you belong to any clubs? That's the sort of thing I need to know so ⁶_____ I can help you find the best job.

All the best,

Uncle John

4 Match the beginnings (1–6) to the correct endings (a–f).

1 Thank you very much — a) really important.

2 I'd really like — b) are music and history.

3 The money is not — c) of the school orchestra and debating society.

4 I'd rather not — d) for your offer.

5 My main interests — e) to get some experience of office work.

6 I'm a member — f) work at the weekend.

5 Write a letter to your uncle telling him about yourself and what kind of work you are interested in.

Dear Uncle John,
Thanks very much for your letter. It's really kind of you to help me …

10a If he had sold the ring, ...

Grammar: Third conditional with *would have*

1 ⭐ **Complete the dialogues with the correct form of the verbs in brackets.**

Leo's bad day!

1 **Leo:** I can't believe I failed my English test. My essay was really good.

 Teacher: Yes, but you didn't write what I asked you to write. If you *had listened* (listen), you *would have passed* (pass).

2 **Leo:** Why aren't I in the school football team?

 Coach: If you _____ (come) to the practice match, I _____ (see) how good you are. I can't choose you if I don't see you play.

3 **Leo:** Why didn't you publish my article in the school newspaper?

 Editor: The newspaper was published today and you gave us your article this morning. If you _____ (give) it to us earlier, we _____ (have) time to put it in the newspaper!

4 **Leo:** I'm starving. I didn't have any lunch at school today.

 Friend: If you _____ (not buy) four packets of crisps, you _____ (have) enough money to buy lunch!

2 ⭐⭐ **Look at the story and complete the sentences.**

Tom's lucky day!

1 Tom's mum/have/more time/not ask/Tom to get the newspaper
 If Tom's mum had had more time, she wouldn't have asked Tom to get the newspaper.

2 Tom's mum/get up/earlier/buy/the newspaper on her way to work

 _____

3 the newsagent's/have/the *Daily News*/Tom/ buy/it there

 _____

4 Tom/not go/to the supermarket/the newsagent/not tell/him to look there

 _____

5 the woman/not drop/her purse/she/enter/ the supermarket before Tom

 _____

6 Tom/not win/the money/the woman/go/in before him

 _____

Vocabulary: Verbs connected with money

3 ★ **Choose the correct options.**

1 How much do you **earn** / **afford** / **inherit** in your job?

2 I can't **repay** / **owe** / **afford** to buy a new dress.

3 Do you **spend** / **lend** / **donate** some of your money to charity?

4 Someone's lost their dog. The **reward** / **debt** / **prize** for finding it is £10.

5 My dad had his own business, but it went **bankrupt** / **owed** / **into debt** last year.

6 Can you **borrow** / **lend** / **donate** me £5 until next week, please?

7 I try to **save** / **owe** / **afford** £100 every month, but it's not always possible.

8 You must be mad to invest **on** / **in** / **to** a company that you know nothing about.

9 Malcolm's crazy! He had £500 and he **spent** / **gave** / **lent** it all away.

10 What are you going to spend your wages **on** / **in** / **for**?

4 ★★★ **Complete the words with one letter in each gap.**

www.helpmewithmymoney.co.uk

Help with your
money problems

Q: I ¹ *l e n t* my friend £5 last month and he hasn't paid it ²b __ __ __ yet. What should I do?

A: You should talk to him. He might have forgotten. I'm sure he doesn't want to ³o __ __ you money.

Q: I got some money as a ⁴r __ __ __ __ __ for being the 'Greenest Student'. My brother wants me to ⁵s __ __ __ it on computer games, but I want to ⁶s __ __ __ it until the holidays. Now he won't let me use his computer. What should I do?

A: You should keep the money. He'll soon forget and let you use his computer again.

Q: My parents got into ⁷d __ __ __ because their business ⁸l __ __ __ money. I want to help them. Are there any good ways I can ⁹m __ __ __ money without working?

A: No, there aren't! You should get a Saturday job. You could ¹⁰e __ __ __ five pounds an hour in a café or shop.

Grammar summary

Third conditional with *would have*

Affirmative

If you **had arrived** earlier, I **would have made** you dinner.

We **would have waited** if you **had phoned** us.

She **would have been** happy **if** she **had passed** her exams.

Negative

I **would have been** on time, **if** I **hadn't got** lost.

If we **had been** quieter, they **wouldn't have heard** us.

If we **hadn't forgotten** the map, we **wouldn't have gone** the wrong way.

Questions and short answers

Would she **have asked** you for help **if** she **hadn't known** the answer?	Yes, she **would (have)**. No, she **wouldn't (have)**.

Note

Use

• We use the third conditional to imagine what would have happened if we had done something differently in the past.
*If I **hadn't been** late, I **would have seen** the film.*

Form

• We form the third conditional using two clauses:
If + past perfect and *would* + *have* + past participle. We separate the two clauses with a comma.
*If you **had told** the truth, you **wouldn't have got** into trouble.*
We can write the two clauses in reverse order without a comma.
*You **wouldn't have got** into trouble **if** you **had told** the truth.*

Common mistakes

~~If I didn't go to school, I would have been in trouble.~~ ✗
If I **hadn't gone** to school, I would have been in trouble. ✓
~~If you hadn't asked me to the party, I wouldn't have went.~~ ✗
If you hadn't asked me to the party, I wouldn't have **gone**. ✓

10b If only we'd had the money!

Vocabulary: Phrasal verbs with out

1 ⬛⬛ **Complete the dialogues with the correct form of the verbs from the box.**

> • leave • sell • turn • throw • work • find
> • ~~eat~~ • point

1 **Anna:** What's for dinner, Mum?

  Mum: We're going to _eat_ out tonight. I'm too tired to cook.

  Anna: There's some chicken in the fridge.

  Mum: No, there isn't. It was very old so I _____ it out.

2 **Teacher:** Sean, your homework isn't very good. You _____ out half the exercises and the ones you did were copied.

  Sean: I couldn't do them, Sir.

  Teacher: I know you find Maths very difficult, but you should try to _____ out the answers for yourself.

  Sean: Yes, Sir.

3 **Natalie:** I went to the theatre to try to get some tickets for the concert before they _____ out, but when I got there, it _____ out that the concert had been cancelled.

  Trish: What a drag!

4 **Headteacher:** I'd just like to _____ out to all the new students that you are not allowed to leave the school playground at break times.

  Student 1: I wonder why he's telling us this now after three weeks.

  Student 2: Maybe he _____ out that Chris and Tom go out to the shops every day.

2 ⬛⬛ **Replace the words in brackets with a phrasal verb from Exercise 1. Make any other necessary changes.**

1 Do you want these old magazines? If you don't, I'll _throw them out_ (put them into the bin).

2 Can you look in the local paper and _____ (see) what time the film starts?

3 We're going to _____ (go to a restaurant) tonight.

4 At the end of the film, it _____ (became clear) that the boy was the girl's long lost brother.

5 What's the answer to number three? I can't _____ (calculate it).

6 You _____ (forgot to include) half the information in your article.

7 I thought my friends had forgotten me, but my mum _____ (let me know) that my mobile phone was switched off.

8 Sorry, we have _____ (sold all our) crisps.

Grammar: wish/if only + past perfect

3 ⬛⬛ **Complete the sentences (1–8) with the past perfect form of the verbs in brackets.**

1 If only we _had played_ (play) better.

2 I wish I _____ (not add) so much salt.

3 I wish I _____ (not spend) so much on CDs.

4 I wish I _____ (not eat) all that cake.

5 If only I _____ (go) to bed earlier.

6 If only I _____ (not take) it to school.

7 If only I _____ (listen) to my teacher.

8 I wish we _____ (bring) a map with us.

4 ⬛⬛⬛ **Read about the famous mistakes. Complete the sentences (1–5) and match them to the correct mistakes (A–E).**

FAMOUS MISTAKES

(A) The first Harry Potter book was rejected by twelve publishers before Bloomsbury Publishing decided to accept it.

(B) In 1984, The Portland Trailblazers had to choose a new basketball player. They chose Sam Bowie and rejected … Michael Jordan, the most famous player in basketball history.

(C) In 1998, Will Smith was offered the part of Neo in *The Matrix*. He rejected it and decided to make *Wild Wild West* instead. *The Matrix* was a huge success, but *Wild Wild West* wasn't very popular.

(D) Andy Murray, the Scottish tennis player, once said that he would support any football team that was playing against England. It made him very unpopular with a lot of English tennis fans.

(E) In 2006, Def Jam Recordings signed a young singer called Stefani Germanotta. Three months later, they decided they didn't want to make CDs with her. She became Lady Gaga.

1 only/we know/how popular the books would be

If only we had known how popular the books
would be.   *A*

2 only/I take/the part instead of Keanu Reeves

_____ ___

3 wish/I not say/that

_____ ___

4 only/we make/a CD with her

_____ ___

5 wish/we not choose/Sam

_____ ___

Grammar summary

wish/if only + past perfect

Affirmative
I **wish/If only** I **had done** more work.
I **wish/If only** they **had phoned** us.
Negative
I **wish/If only** we **hadn't forgotten** the food.
I **wish/If only** I **hadn't missed** the last train.

Note

Use

- We use *wish/if only* + past perfect to show that we regret something that happened or didn't happen in the past and would have liked it to have been different.
  *I wish I **hadn't given up** learning French.*
  *If only we **had asked** for directions.*

- We can use *wish/if only* + past perfect with the third conditional to explain why we wish things had been different.
  *I **wish** I **had worked** harder. **If** I **had worked** harder, I **would have done** better in my exams.*
  *If only I **hadn't spent** all my money. **If** I **hadn't spent** all my money, I **would go out** tonight.*

Common mistakes

~~If only I didn't go to bed late last night.~~ ✗
If only I **hadn't gone** to bed late last night. ✓
~~I wish we had a video camera when the children were young.~~ ✗
I wish we **had had** a video camera when the children were young. ✓

10c I might not have done so well.

Phrases

1 🔲 **Complete the dialogue with the phrases from the box.**

> • Tell me about it! • That's such a pain!
> • ~~What are you up to~~ • Lead the way!
> • It's on me. • How about it?

Tom: Hey, Harry! ¹*What are you up to* this afternoon?

Harry: Nothing much. I haven't got any money. Going out is so expensive.

Tom: ² _____ I spent £10 last Friday on nothing.

Harry: Oh dear, have you got any money left?

Tom: A little.

Harry: What shall we do?

Tom: We could go to Mario's.
³ _____ Don't worry about money. ⁴ _____

Harry: Great. ⁵ _____ Wait a minute. I'll just tell my mum. Mum, I'm just going out with Tom.

Mum: Sorry, dear. I have to go out. You'll have to look after your little brother.

Harry: Oh no! ⁶ _____

Tom: Never mind. Another time. See you later. Have fun with your little brother!

Grammar: Third conditional with *might have*

2 🔲 **Complete the dialogues with the correct form of the verbs in brackets.**

1 Jake: What a terrible match. I can't believe we lost 3–0. If Martin *had played* (play), we *might have won* (might win).

Luke: If Martin _____ (be) in the team, we _____ (might lose) 4–0! He sometimes plays really badly.

2 Nathan: If you _____ (arrive) earlier, we _____ (might get) tickets for the concert.

Charles: They _____ (might sell) out even if I _____ (arrive) at 8 a.m., but I bought two tickets on the internet last night!

3 Jenny: It's a shame you couldn't come to the party on Saturday. If you _____ (come), you _____ (might meet) someone nice.

Tanya: Yes, but if I _____ (not meet) anyone nice, I _____ (might spend) all evening on my own!

4 Simon: So, what did you think of the film, Leo?

Leo: Well, it was a bit difficult to follow.

Simon: Yes. I know what you mean. If you _____ (read) the book, you _____ (might understand) the film.

Leo: If I _____ (read) the book, I _____ (might not go) to see the film at all.

5 Debbie: If you _____ (check) the time of the film on the internet, we _____ (might not miss) the start.

Rob: Yes, but if I _____ (switch on) my computer, I _____ (might not leave) the house at all!

3 🔲 **Look at the information about the celebrities. Complete the sentences about what they might have done.**

Mick Jagger
He studied at the London School of Economics.
not join/The Rolling Stones/ become/businessman

1 If Mick Jagger *hadn't joined The Rolling Stones, he might have become* a businessman.

Roger Federer
When he was young, he was really good at football.
play football for Basel FC/ not play/tennis

2 Roger Federer _____ _____ tennis.

80

Victoria Beckham
She wanted to become a star when she saw the film *Fame*.
not see/*Fame*/not want/to be a star

3 If Victoria Beckham _____
_____ to be a star.

Brad Pitt
He studied Journalism at the University of Missouri.
become a journalist/not start/acting

4 Brad Pitt _____
_____ acting.

Use your English: Give and accept congratulations

4 ⭐ **Complete the words.**

Dialogue 1:

Lisa: You'll never ¹g*uess* ! I've been chosen to play the lead part in the school play.

Jackie: Well ²d_____! That's ³f_____.

Lisa: Thanks. I never believed it would ⁴h_____. I couldn't have done it ⁵w_____ you. You gave me the confidence to try acting.

Jackie: Don't be ⁶s_____. I ⁷_____ you could do it. You just needed someone to make you see how talented you are.

Dialogue 2:

Keith: ⁸B_____ it or not, my parents have bought me a new computer.

Sam: Wow! ⁹T_____ great!

Keith: It must have been my ¹⁰l_____ day.

Sam: Well, you ¹¹d_____ it. You help them a lot with their business. You work for them almost every Saturday.

Keith: That's true. Hey, let's go and ¹²c_____. Pizza is on me.

Grammar summary

Third conditional with *might have*

Affirmative

If I **had learned** French, I **might have moved** to France.
If she **had asked** someone for help, she **might have arrived** earlier.

Negative

They **might have worked out** the answer together if they **hadn't had** an argument.
We **might not have missed** the plane if you **hadn't stopped** to buy a drink.

Note

Use

- See Unit 10a page 77 for uses of the third conditional.
- We can use *might* instead of *would* to give a possible past result of a past situation or event because it isn't always possible to say what would definitely have happened.
  *If I **had worn** my black suit, I **might have got** the job.*
  *If you **hadn't eaten** chips just before your tennis match, you **might have won**.*

Form

- We form the third conditional with *might* using two clauses:
  If + past perfect and *might* + *have* + past participle.
  We separate the two clauses with a comma.
  *If the test **had been** easier, I **might have** passed.*
- We can write the two clauses in reverse order without a comma.
  *I **might have passed** the test **if** it **had been** easier.*

Common mistakes

~~*If I didn't finish my homework, the teacher might have written to my parents.*~~ ✗
*If I **hadn't finished** my homework, the teacher might have written to my parents.* ✓
~~*If I had had more time, I might have went out.*~~ ✗
*If I had had more time, I might have **gone** out.* ✓

10 Language round-up

1 Complete the sentences with the words from the box.

> • pointed • work • if • sold • would • ~~wish~~
> • threw • left • only • eaten • had (x2) • found

Man: I hate cooking! I ¹*wish* we had
² _____ out this evening.

Joe: That new sofa you bought is too big.

Bob: Well, I wish you ³_____
⁴_____ that out earlier!

Girl: If ⁵_____ you had ⁶_____
out the time of the film before we left
home!

Man: I can't ⁷_____ out how to use this.
I wish I ⁸_____ the instructions.

Woman: You probably ⁹_____ them out!

Shop assistant: I'm sorry. We've just ¹⁰_____
out of *Iron Man* DVDs.

Girl: ¹¹_____ only we had ¹²_____
home earlier, we ¹³_____ have got
one.

.../12

2 Make full sentences and questions from the prompts.

Stephanie Meyer's first choice for Edward in
the *Twilight* films was Henry Cavill, but he was
twenty-five when they started making the films.

1 Henry/be younger/they might/choose him

   If Henry had been younger, they might have
   chosen him.

2 Henry/play/Edward, what films/Robert
Pattinson/be in?

   _____

3 Kristen Stewart/fall in love/with Henry/if he play/
Edward?

   _____

4 Robert/not be/in the film/it be/so popular?

   _____

José Mourinho left Chelsea in 2007. He managed
Real Madrid before returning to Chelsea in 2013.

5 Chelsea/be/more successful/if José/stay there?

   _____

6 José/not go/to Real Madrid/Chelsea might/win/
the Champions League.

   _____

7 José/not return/to Chelsea/who/be/their new
manager in 2013?

   _____

8 Real Madrid/be happy/if José/stay?

   _____

.../14

3 Choose the correct options.

We all have regrets. I remember when I ¹(**threw**) /
sold / **turned** out an old jumper and, a few weeks
later, I wanted to wear it. Or the time when I
decided to buy tickets to a big football match, but
they had ²**given** / **thrown** / **sold** out before I got
there. These were small things, though. Now, I'm
twenty and very unhappy.

When I had to decide what to do at university, I
wish I ³**listened** / **had listened** / **would listen** to
my parents. I thought I knew best, but it ⁴**worked** /
turned / **found** out that I didn't. I didn't ⁵**turn** /
find / **make** that out until I got to university. I wish
I ⁶**would have** / **have** / **had** read more about the
course. If I had, I ⁷**had known** / **would know** /
would have known more about it.

The other regret I've got is to do with money. My
parents always tried to get me to ⁸**save** / **owe** /
borrow money, but I never did. My parents ⁹**lent** /
borrowed / **owed** me £2,000 for university, but
I spent most of it on having fun and ¹⁰**working** /
eating / **cooking** out in restaurants. Now I ¹¹**owe** /
borrow / **lend** them money and have to pay it
¹²**back** / **out** / **down**. I found a part-time job in a
restaurant. I don't ¹³**pay** / **earn** / **donate** much, but
I can ¹⁴**afford** / **repay** / **spend** to give my parents
£20 a week so, in two years, I won't be in debt
anymore! If only I ¹⁵**was** / **have been** / **had been**
more sensible when I first got here.

.../14

🔊 15 **LISTEN AND CHECK YOUR SCORE**	
Total	.../40

10 Skills practice

SKILLS FOCUS: READING, LISTENING AND WRITING

Read

1 📖 **Read the text quickly. Choose the correct options.**

1 Alice is moving to …	a) Egypt.	b) Kenya.	c) Argentina.
2 Steve lives in …	a) Egypt.	b) Kenya.	c) Argentina.
3 Theresa's friend is from …	a) Egypt.	b) Kenya.	c) Argentina.

www.expatkids_info_exchange.com/forum

Hi. My family is moving to Kenya for a year. Can anyone give me some guidelines on social customs? *Alice, aged 15*

You'll love Kenya, Alice. It's a beautiful country. Don't be surprised by lots of questions! If you are invited to a Kenyan home, you should take cakes, sweets or flowers. Try to remember to give them to your host with your right hand or both hands. You should always wash your hands before you eat. Try to finish everything on your plate and have fun!
Barack, aged 16

I'm living in Egypt and my Egyptian friend has invited me to dinner at his house. I'm a bit nervous. Please help! *Steve, aged 14*

I've lived in Egypt for six years. When you eat dinner, always leave some food on your plate. After dinner you will get black tea. You shouldn't stay long after this. It means it is time for you to go home. *Ahmed, aged 15*

Can anyone help me? I'm going to dinner at my friend's house. She's Argentinian. Any tips? *Theresa, aged 15*

Hi, Theresa. Firstly, look as smart as you can. Wear a dress or a skirt and blouse. You shouldn't arrive on time. Come thirty minutes late – really – and take a small present. You should leave a little bit of food on your plate. When you leave, say goodbye to everyone individually. Shake their hands. Start with the oldest first. Have a good meal! *Tia, aged 15*

2 **Read the texts again and match the customs to the countries. Write K (Kenya), E (Egypt) or A (Argentina).**

1 People ask you lots of questions. [K]
2 You ought to finish everything. [ ]
3 You should wear smart clothes. [ ]
4 Presents should not be given with your left hand. [ ]
5 Shake everyone's hand when you leave. [ ]
6 It is easy to know when you should leave. [ ]
7 Cakes make a good present. [ ]

Listen

3 🎧 16 **Listen and number the stages (a–d) in the order that they happen.**

a) The routine. [ ]   c) The shock. [ ]
b) The holiday. [1]   d) The worry. [ ]

4 🎧 16 **Listen again and write true (T) or false (F).**

1 Luke was unhappy when he arrived. [F]
2 He has been in Japan for six months. [ ]
3 Luke's problem is not very common. [ ]
4 Luke should be happier soon. [ ]
5 The last problem won't affect him in Japan. [ ]
6 Luke's mother read about culture shock problems before she went to Japan. [ ]

Write

5 **Imagine a friend from a different country is coming on an exchange visit. Write a letter about the social customs and rules in your home and school they might find strange.**

Dear …
I'm really excited about your visit. Before you arrive, I want to tell you a little about my home life and what it's like in our school so that you aren't too surprised …

Notes

Notes

Pearson Education Limited
Edinburgh Gate
Harlow
Essex CM20 2JE
England
and Associated Companies throughout the world.

www.english.com/livebeat

© Pearson Education Limited 2015

This impression published 2015

ISBN: 978-1-4477-5301-2

Set in Helvetica Neue LT Std 55 Roman 10/14pt

ARP impression 98

Printed by Ashford Colour Press Ltd.

Illustration Acknowledgements

(Key: b-bottom; c-centre; l-left; r-right; t-top)

Illustrated by David Banks pages 4, 16, 30, 40, 48, 76; Joanna Kerr pages 20, 29 (top left), 36 (right), 41; Pat Murray (Graham-Cameron Illustration) pages 8 (top), 14, 63, 73; Anita Romeo (Advocate Art)

Photo Acknowledgements

The publisher would like to thank the following for their kind permission to reproduce their photographs:

(Key: b-bottom; c-centre; l-left; r-right; t-top)

Alamy Images: Pawel Libera Images 49; **Corbis:** Kevin Fleming 65, Jim Reed Photography - Severe & 38; **Fotolia.com:** BlueSkyImages 61; **Getty Images:** AFP / Sebastian Willnow 68t, Chris Jackson 43, Mike Pont 27, Stringer / Tasos Katopodis 33; **Pearson Education:** 39; **Press Association Images:** Empics Entertainment / ABACA USA / Lionel Hahn 12; **Reuters:** Rick Wilking 14; **Rex Features:** 7b, 81b, Jason Bye 24, Juergen Hasenkopf 80b, Jen Lowery 7bc, MCP 81t, Brian Rasic 7tc, Sipa Press 7t, Michael Williams 80t; **The Kobal Collection:** Columbia / Paramount / Wingnut / Amblin 52br, Fox 2000 Pictures / Dune Entertainment / Ingenious Media / Haishang Films 52tr, Jerry Bruckheimer Films 52tc, Marvel / Paramount 52tl, New Line Cinema 52bl, Riama-Pathe-Gray / Astor-AIP 68b

All other images © Pearson Education

Cover images: *Front:* **Shutterstock.com:** ayakovlevcom